ENTER[PRISE] ARCHITECTURE MADE SIMPLE

Using the Ready, Set, Go Approach to Achieving Information Centricity

first edition

Håkan Edvinsson and Lottie Aderinne

Published by:
Technics Publications, LLC
2 Lindsley Road
Basking Ridge, NJ 07920 USA

http://www.TechnicsPub.com

Cover design by Mark Brye
Illustrations by Björn Nilsson

Edited by Elizabeth Bernat and Carol Lehn

ISBN, print ed.   978-1-935504-63-4
ISBN, Kindle ed. 978-1-935504-64-1
ISBN, ePub ed.   978-1-935504-65-8

First Printing 2013

Library of Congress Control Number: 2013952942

Table of Contents

Introduction

An enterprise is an ecosystem, a web of interrelated entities including people, processes, resources, information, and IT systems. Enterprises are among the most complicated systems ever created by man. In fact, their level of complexity is so great that a complete understanding of them may be beyond our grasp.

Nevertheless, in order to effectively manage an enterprise, you need to make an accurate map of its components and relationships. This map will be the ubiquitous language among all parties working within the enterprise, the shared view of what you have and where you want to go. If you do not know what you are working with, you cannot easily make adjustments when reacting to changes in demand or to the arrival of new opportunities. Without a comprehensive map, you may not be able to detect or assess what is happening before you are overrun with problems.

Enterprise architecture is about mastering the entirety of the enterprise's environment. By "entirety," we mean not only the organization itself, but the whole world in which it operates as well as the other people and businesses on which it depends. It is a challenge to maintain control of an entire enterprise and keep its different functions working together correctly while the organization is constantly changing. Often, the majority of the employees are focused exclusively on their own part of the enterprise, and the CEO is trying to manage everything from the top.

The enterprise architect supplements traditional organizational responsibilities by filling an important gap: keeping track of what each person needs to do and making sure that neglected-but-necessary tasks are completed. Enterprise architects help to keep overall aspects of an enterprise working efficiently together even in the face of significant changes. They can determine how a business improvement or innovation in one part of the company will affect other sectors, eliminate redundancies in different areas of management, and arrange the most cost-effective way to schedule planned activities.

To accomplish all of these tasks, the enterprise architect needs to be aware of the purpose and function of each of the business's processes, the information that is produced and used by the business, and the processes' supporting functions. Typically, an enterprise architect knows whether or not the company has properly set up their information systems. If the company has not, which is usually the case, the architect should have a roadmap for how to move to a suitable landscape of information systems.

Enterprise architecture has been the subject of many works. There are ontologies to help to classify elements of the enterprise as well as high-level frameworks that try to impose semantics on every area of knowledge or work methodology that can be considered enterprise architecture. These manuals have their value, but they are largely theoretical and heavy-footed. Their pages are lacking in practical applications and do not tell you anything about daily work as an enterprise architect.

Our message about enterprise architecture is different in several ways:

- It gives you directions on how to institute and implement enterprise architecture in your organization. You can make a quick start and establish a baseline for your enterprise architecture in about ten weeks, then grow and stabilize the architecture over time. You will be able to build close relationships with stakeholders and delivery teams, but you will not need to micromanage the architecture's operations.

- It emphasizes that enterprise architecture is about business, not information technology. A business's processes and information are business assets; even information systems are business assets and are treated as such. Enterprise architecture is not merely business-driven; it also targets the business and is therefore business-oriented the whole way through. This book shows you how to involve the business community and foster collaboration between the business and IT sectors in developing the architecture.

- It is in a form to initiate and facilitate dramatic business development. The architecture of an enterprise must be tolerant of currently unknown business initiatives.

- It shows you how to get a holistic view of the process of implementing enterprise architecture. Most other enterprise architecture methods focus on details while failing to provide an architectural overview that is understandable by non-IT professionals.

- It recognizes that information is a key business asset and that information architecture is a key part of the enterprise architecture.

- It is concise. It does not pretend to cover all you need to know; rather, it gives you the information that is most important for effective and successful guidance. Sometimes, less is more.

- It is based on real experience. The book is based on 30 years of work in the enterprise architecture field by the authors, our colleagues in Europe, customer cases, and our students.

This book is for those who are somewhat familiar with enterprise architecture and the organizational paradigm it challenges. If your company is about to make a major change and you are looking for a way to reduce the changes into manageable pieces—and still retain control of how they fit together—this is your handbook. Maybe you are already acting as an enterprise architect and using a formal method, but you need practical hints. Or maybe you are about to set up an enterprise architect network or group of specialists and need input on how to organize your work.

HOW TO DERIVE THE ARCHITECTURE AND ITS GOVERNANCE

So, what's the secret? How do you manage to describe, improve, and implement an endeavor as complex and large as enterprise architecture? We use a simple architecture method based on the following principles, which will be further developed later in this book:

- Embrace your business information structure, and base your enterprise architecture on it. An information structure reflects business rules by expressing the relationships between important concepts. For instance, while a customer may place one or more customer orders, a customer order may be placed by just one customer. Describing your business information structure in such a manner will reveal lots of rules, both universal, as in this generic example, as well as completely unique. So derive the architecture structure from the way your business information is structured.

- Do not define your business information structure so that it is dependent of your IT system structures and organizational influences. Instead, define and relate each entity in your information structure based on the context from which the business information originates. That is, define "customer" from the business circumstances under which someone becomes one.

- Base your ideal architecture roadmap on the order in which business information originates. For example, customer and product information must be in place before a customer order can be taken. This is the natural way of placing a customer's order. No one builds the roof for a house before raising the walls, and the foundation must be ready before the walls go up. When it comes to IT solutions, this common-sense sequence of acquiring information is often ignored.

- Form the architecture governance according to the same principle. That is, find owners of common business concepts, such as "customer," "product," and "customer order," that are close to where the business concept originates. For instance, information about new customers will typically be captured, and thus originate, within the sales or customer relations section of the organization. So in this case, you would assign the ownership of "customer" to a manager in the customer relations part of the organization. The closer you are to the information's origination point, the more you understand the conditions and business rules that apply when the information is captured. This principle allows you to allocate ownership of architectural assets in a way that is neutral to the organizational structure.

WHAT IS THE PROBLEM?

In reality, most businesses are stuck in environments where change is sluggish, impeding the desired level of flexibility. Figure A shows a *poor* information cycle. Its problems will increase unless the circle is broken.

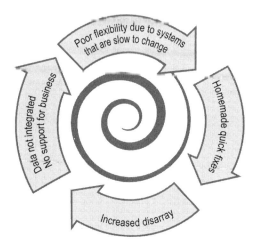

Figure A   A poor information cycle.

Source: "Disparate data cycle" adapted from Michael Brackett. Used with permission.

One of the causes of the problems in Figure A is that IT support has frequently been based on the needs of individual organizations or departments without an overall perspective and without being connected to business development. Imagine if, instead, we could identify something more stable than the organization on which to base our IT support. We believe that the most stable aspect of an enterprise is its information structure. Almost anything else around us will change eventually.

Consider your own company's organizational structure. When was the last time it was changed, and how much time passed since the change before that? An organization chart is not a stable base for a long-term architecture. It is also important to consider your business processes; will we continue doing things as we are doing them today? Or will we have the freedom to reorganize the processes? If we want to improve the quality of our products and services, increase operational performance, or start doing something new, we have to change our business processes. We expect the processes to be flexible rather than stable. Forming the enterprise architecture from the current process structure is therefore a hopeless task since we will soon be trying to run new processes in obsolete process tracks. The information structure, however, does not change as long as we are running the same kind of business. The three structure types—organization, process, and information—can be illustrated graphically and are easy to redesign with a simple remodeling effort. As shown in Figure B, the information structure will experience small changes, such as in regards to its size, but it will not change dramatically. The information structure is where the most sustainable architecture basis exists.

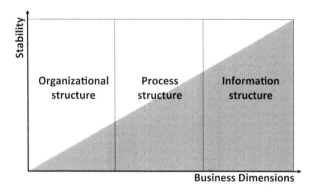

Figure B   Three dimensions of an enterprise: organizational, process and information. Structures with greater stability are more suitable bases for an enterprise architecture.

When establishing a city, planning is based around essential construction projects such as residential areas, schools, airports, and roads. To achieve an efficient and practical city, individuals and companies are not allowed to start building without first obtaining a building permit. The same approach should be taken to generate support for an enterprise. That is, a city plan should show, at a general level, which changes are needed. Each individual initiative for new functionality should be checked against the city plan and coordinated with one another to prevent redundant work. Throughout the book, we will use the term "city plan" to represent this perspective.

READY, SET, GO OVERVIEW

The Ready-Set-Go method for introducing enterprise architecture provides you, the enterprise architect, with an immediate understanding of the basic steps for starting, organizing, and operating the entirety of your organization's architecture.

Since the Ready-Set Go method is a start-up process, we have chosen to describe it with a process description. Usually, a process description suggests who should carry out each step. As we do not want to be overly specific, we will describe only what should be done and what result should be produced. Therefore, when you execute these processes, see the Ready-Set-Go method as being driven by a chief enterprise architect who allows each step to be carried out by the best available specialist.

In this book, we will present a method that shows the following:

Chapter 1: *Ready* shows how to model and analyze your business operations, assess their current status, construct a future scenario, compare it to the current structure, analyze what you see, and show the result in a city plan. *Ready* produces insight into the degree of redundancy in the business's operations and highlights possible shortcomings in the quality of its information. It also provides a plan of action based on the insights thus obtained. Chapter 1 is about understanding your enterprise's business and its need for improved architecture, both of which are summarized in a "city plan" that is based on your observations and requirements. This is the awareness step of enterprise architecture maturity.

Chapter 2: *Set* deals with preparing for the implementation of the architecture with governance, enterprise architecture organization, staffing, etc. This is the organizing step before beginning the actual work.

Chapter 3: *Go* establishes how to implement a city plan in practice. It deals with the practicalities of working as an enterprise architect and is called the "running" step.

The common thread through all aspects of the enterprise architect's work is the architect's mastery of a number of tools, such as business models, process models, information models, and matrices. The process followed by the enterprise architect is described simply in this book in terms of the sequence Ready-Set-Go, in which the initiation of the process is crucial to its success. The whole method is summarized in Figure C.

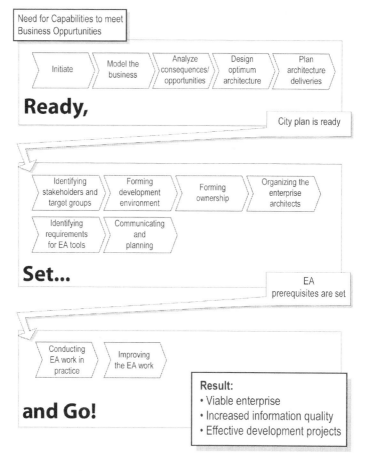

Figure C   Ready, Set and Go overview.

We address how to initiate the architecture process within the organization in such a way that the overarching enterprise architecture and architecture-driven approach can be applied methodically and gradually improved.

Our method is consistent with the Zachman Framework 3.0. The **Appendix**, *Frameworks*, provides an overview of how the Zachman Framework is applied.

CONVENTIONS USED IN THIS BOOK

In this book, methods are outlined in general terms so that they can be adapted to suit all sectors and types of enterprise architecture initiatives. For this reason, diagrams take the same graphical form regardless of the reasons for improving the architecture. Keep in mind that the perspective and angle of approach in the contents of the architecture will be completely different if they are motivated by business development as opposed to an IT-focused augmentation.

Throughout the book, we use the abbreviation EA to denote enterprise architecture.

All of the business model diagram examples in the book describe the architecture of a fictional company called BestBoatBuilder.com. This company is a web-based retailer for boating enthusiasts and provides supplies for both professional and leisure purposes. Anyone who needs accessories or spare parts for smaller boats will find the right item at this site. The company has been around for five years and was formed without a planned architecture. Now it wishes to expand; their intention is to increase sales by between 10 and 100 times and become a global company in a controlled way.

ABOUT THE AUTHORS

The authors have combined more than three decades of experience in enterprise architecture, business development, and business modeling. They have introduced enterprise architecture to numerous different sectors and areas of operations. Both have been active as consultants and educators; they have also been examiners for a training course that certifies enterprise architects. In these roles, they have established the foundations of the enterprise architecture concept for numerous individuals and businesses.

Edvinsson is currently the CTO and partner of Informed Decisions and Aderinne is the owner and partner of Vilante Consulting. Both companies provide consulting services for EA and change management projects.

Chapter 1
READY

Summary of activities in *Ready*:

Initiating the assignment:
- Identifying purpose and awareness
- Obtaining executive sponsorship and management commitment
- Involving participants
- Calculating risks.

Modeling the business processes and information:
- Modeling enterprise processes
- Modeling the business information structure of the enterprise
- Expressing business expectations
- Linking processes, business objectives, and customer values.

Analyzing consequences and opportunities:
- Identifying entity groups
- Determining information life cycle type
- Describing process' need of information
- Describing existing systems
- Analyzing opportunities and assessing benefits.

Designing the optimum architecture:
- Designing the ideal architecture using business capabilities
- Understanding the process and systems matrices
- Forming ideal blocks in the architecture matrix
- Forming a realistic architecture.

Planning the enterprise architecture deliverables:
- Planning the implementation of EA in the short term
- Planning the implementation of EA in the long term
- Establishing a roadmap
- Compiling the city plan.

CITY PLAN BASIC ELEMENTS

The first step of the enterprise architecture process, in which we form the city plan, provides a strategy for reorganizing the business so that it can be improved and meet new challenges quickly and painlessly. The city plan consists of descriptions about the business's baseline and target state, as well as information about how it will move from the baseline to the target state. This plan is not only a transition plan for the organization, for it also includes a delivery plan for the operative enterprise architects.

A city plan is comprised of general descriptions of business processes (the way we do things) and information structures (what knowledge we use and produce), as well as analyses of the connections between these two groups. By analyzing how well current systems support the processes, the city plan can highlight any shortcomings in the current systems portfolio and, therefore, suggest the best way to improve it. Accordingly, the city plan will be your enterprise architecture plan.

The city plan typically contains a description of the business in the form of both process and information structure diagrams. These diagrams are combined with current systems, as well as planned future systems, so that everything is displayed graphically in several matrices. As seen in Figure 1.1, the basic elements of the architecture come from three perspectives: processes, information, and systems. These perspectives are combined by using three matrices that display the information needed by the processes, the systems' contents, and the systems' information supply.

Based on analyses of the business and its systems, the ideal enterprise architecture can be proposed. This is used for deciding which processes should be improved, which systems should be developed or phased out, and the order in which these changes should take place. Enterprises need the stable platform provided by the ideal systems structure to be able to cope with truly dramatic changes and to be able to derive the full benefit from the businesses' knowledge and information assets.

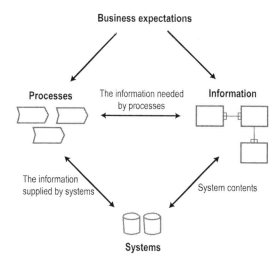

Figure 1.1   The basic elements of a city plan.

The EA process achieves its greatest success with solid support from enterprise management and the active participation of business operations representatives. Both of these groups contribute valuable knowledge about the priorities, targets, and visions of the business while providing the EA process with the solid foundation it requires as efforts progress.

Forming a city plan consists of the following steps:

1. Initiating the assignment
2. Modeling the business processes and information
3. Analyzing consequences and opportunities
4. Designing the optimum architecture
5. Planning the enterprise architecture deliverables.

The first three steps are usually carried out over a period of two to three months. The last two steps, architecture design and EA planning, should normally take two to three weeks. If it is impossible to stay within this timeframe, the scope of the EA project is probably too wide.

As stated in the introduction, the process of forming the city plan should be driven by a chief enterprise architect or, if one is not available, a person who has the skills to become one. Most of the steps in this EA method are addressed to those who are actively working to bring EA into their organization. However, there are some procedures that call for certain expertise, such as business modeling.

1.1 INITIATING THE ASSIGNMENT

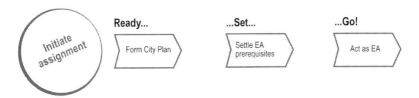

Figure 1.2   The EA process method focusing on initiation.

Before embarking on the architecture process, it is important to ensure that the correct conditions are in place in order for the process to be successful. Therefore, it is necessary to work through the various initiation stages at the beginning of the architecture assignment. At the end of this "Initiation" stage, you will have answers to the following questions:

- Why should we do this?
- Is everybody aware of why?
- Who takes responsibility for the problem, is affected by the problem, or will benefit from solving the problem?
- Who should participate?
- What are the risks?
- Are there ongoing parallel activities to consider?
- Are there previous results we can reuse?
- What are the key success factors for this kind of work?

Purpose of EA and EA awareness

Start with talking about why interest in enterprise architecture has increased in the business to such an extent that a collective effort is required. What are the expectations of management and the affected business areas? The external and internal expectations about the results of the initiative form the guideline for the people involved in EA work.

Common reasons for starting an EA initiative include the following:

- A business opportunity, such as a huge expansion or a significant innovation, has such an influence on the organization that an overview and partial or total makeover of the business structure is required. Existing processes and systems are simply not capable of keeping up with the planned changes. Here, EA is at its best. Picture the ideal setup of the process and the information and systems combination, and make a city plan to get to your desired destination.

- After years of difficulties in executing continuous changes, quality improvements, or growth, a new requirement arises that proves to be too much for the business to keep up with. The problem the business now faces is how to decide on the best spot to start making improvements. Using the analysis from the "Ready" steps gives you the knowledge to make that decision. Also, the origins of this mess will be revealed.

- The systems that are the spine of the business are starting to crack due to technical reasons. A major replacement is inevitable, but the existing legacy system is typically based on outdated technology that has little documentation and a shortage of specialists. Again, the "Ready" method will guide you through making a proper roadmap for this challenge.

- Modern technical environments and development methods are great, but not entirely enough. The overall roadmap is missing. A city plan from the "Ready" chapter will provide that roadmap.

The result from the "Ready" step is a plan for how to meet these challenges. Be sure to formulate the reasons for implementing the EA process carefully and remember that enterprise architecture is just a part of the solution. Here are two examples of how to state, to the entire organization, the reasons for using EA:

- Business expectation: "The market for our products is growing tremendously in Asia. We have 15% of the market share in Europe today. We need our company to be twice as big in the next ten years to keep the same market share percentage in Asia, as that market is growing tremendously." EA challenge: Form a setup that allows us to double our daily volume without doubling the problems and costs we have today.

- Business expectation: "Every time we launch a new product, we need to perform a significant amount of manual work to update many systems. Even with updates, these systems are better fitted for managing our old products." EA challenge: Form a plan to move the business towards the ideal architecture. Let the plan address the lifecycle of the product and make sure that it includes our valuable aftermarket.

The pace of architecture implementation is not determined solely by the level of ambition and the availability of resources. If time is a main concern, it is necessary to be pragmatic and prioritize the steps set out in this method. It may also be necessary to complete the steps in a different order than is proposed in this book.

Establish who will receive the city plan and how they will chart their progress. This information will determine the scope, design, level of detail, and focus of the EA material. Contact the receiving person(s) and agree on what to deliver, in what form, detail level, and when. It is critical to have concrete expectations regarding the results expected from the project. If the city plan recipient is a project team implementing a major system change, they should not be expected to simply complete tasks associated with that project. The EA process has a far longer time horizon compared to a single project.

Establish a clear picture of the challenges facing people in the organization. It is easier to gain people's respect and commitment for the EA process if the need for it is well understood and convincing. If there is not a broad awareness of the reason for developing an enterprise architecture, extra energy will need to be devoted to motivating participants. Instilling motivation for EA in all workers requires sending out carefully worded invitations to participate in meetings, broadcasting the attendance of a senior manager at major workshops, making educational presentation materials easily available, and having a project manager who is continuously prepared to persuade participants of the importance of continuing the EA process.

It is a good idea to gain a general feel for the level of EA awareness in the organization. To what extent do the executive sponsor, project managers, and key participants understand the EA concept? It is not necessary for everyone to have in-depth knowledge, but if sponsors and project managers have previously been involved in architecture assignments, they will already be convinced of EA's benefits and less work will be required to make major participants enthusiastic about the project. Previous knowledge provides conditions for a smoother process for the enterprise architect, who can then focus on forming an architecture.

Executive sponsor and management commitment

Your architectural endeavors will be more successful if you develop a city plan with a formal executive sponsor. Architecture assignments, in particular, require an especially strong executive sponsor. The scope of these assignments is broader than for other development projects and will cut across the entire organization. Therefore, there must be clarity in regards to who is guiding the project and what it involves. Your EA assignment will be most successful if the executive sponsor has an interest in its underlying expectations as well as a clear understanding of how their business will benefit from EA. It is an advantage if this person also enjoys a high level of credibility throughout the organization.

The executive sponsor must be able to engage other management representatives in the reorganization effort and assist the architect in encouraging these individuals to participate in a number of activities. It is a good idea to form a strategic team that includes management representatives (preferably including the CEO) and other people with the ability and vision to see new opportunities. This group should meet regularly throughout the architecture process to update each other about issues affecting the business, the focus of efforts, and adjustments to the target scenario. As work proceeds, seek approval from this group on key results such as process maps, strategy alignment, important concepts, and the long-term goals of the architecture process.

It may be sufficient for the strategic team to set aside an average of two or three hours every other week during the course of the architecture assignment. However, during the first half of the assignment, you should meet with the group more frequently to ensure that the right conditions are established from the beginning. These meetings can also be used to discuss how work will continue once the city plan has been completed.

Normally, management is not as interested in architecture as is the enterprise architect, since they have numerous other issues to contend with. Consequently, make sure that the meetings are interesting for management and exciting to be a part of. A good way to make this happen is to use a current problem on management's agenda as your starting point.

Participants

Organize company participation with the help of the executive sponsor. Staff the project team with a project manager, an architect, and one or two workshop facilitators. Form a workshop group with knowledgeable representatives from different business areas. Gaining access to these people's knowledge is critical, and their time needs to be booked early. Consequently, the manager of the architecture project should set dates for workshops and other vital activities as early as possible to ensure full participation and sufficient meeting space. Send out invitations to attend workshops and key working meetings at least four weeks in advance and enlist the sponsor's help in ensuring that participants are able to set time aside to attend the meetings.

Make sure that the workshop participants will be actively involved throughout the city planning process. Introducing new members to the workshop group along the way can easily slow down the working pace since they will need to be brought up to speed on what has been developed by the other group members. The workshop group should have between 10 and 20 members and include business knowledge from the entire scope of the architecture. The project team may be staffed with one or two business representatives from the workshop group. If some members are part of both groups, they can give the project business input and help resolve minor issues as it progresses.

Ideally, the participants in the workshops should be identical at all meetings. However, it is sometimes necessary to call in a specialist to address a particular area. Carry out the meeting with the specialist with a smaller group of participants for a shorter length of time and then make a report to the full group at the next workshop. Combined, these measures make it easier to maintain cohesion of the results between workshops as the process progresses.

Involve participants in tasks between the workshops. Have them formulate or compile various business descriptions and definitions as the project proceeds. Others in their network of contacts can also help by complementing and contributing to the quality of the results.

As shown in Figure 1.3, you will need to form four teams:

1. The **Steering committee** deals with common project steering issues and usually meets once every second month. The primary purpose with this group is to govern the project.

2. The **Strategy group** meets for between one and two hours every second week in the beginning and once a month after three or four meetings. The purpose of this team is to both resolve major business issues and raise EA awareness in the management level.

3. The **Workshop group** takes eight to ten workshop days to organize and make improvements to the target architecture. The purpose of this group is to collect accurate and important knowledge about business operations. This is also a reference group for resolving minor issues.

4. The **Project team** is the core team that performs the actual work. They work on the city plan for at least 50% of their time during the first two to three months.

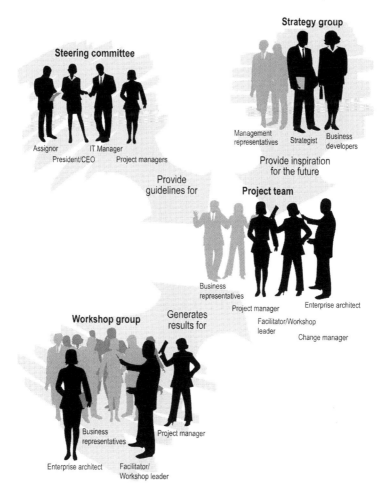

Figure 1.3   Proposed project organization for the forming of a city plan.

Risks

EA projects are exposed to more risks than are other projects, especially during the first EA attempt within the organization. The most significant risks are discussed below.

- **Lack of management support**. Any reorganization of the enterprise during the planned execution of the project will affect the architecture process. For example, new decision makers may question the process and be tempted to withdraw from opportunities for participants to continue their work on the architecture. It is by establishing support among management that an architecture process can survive reorganization. Therefore, be certain to enlist into the architecture development process more than one member of top-level management, or at least senior management, who understand the benefits of improving the architecture.

- **No proven track record**. Having a sponsor is essential to the success of the effort, as is his or her confidence in those carrying out the architecture process. So, paradoxically, the first time you carry out a major architecture process, it will be helpful to have previously been involved in several such projects. Enlist the help of a senior architect colleague to help you carry out the most important steps.

- **Insecure sponsor**. If the sponsor requires all communication to pass through him or her, it may be an indication that that person is uncertain of his or her role, has interests other than the objectives of the architecture process, or is uncertain of the architect's capability. Regardless of the reason, the sponsor must allow the project manager and architect to take the leading roles in the project so that no one wastes time and energy that could have been better spent elsewhere. Try to establish independence in the workplace, along with the sponsor's confidence.

- **Counter-productive executive decisions**. Management is constantly taking the initiative and making decisions on a wide variety of issues. It may be the case that although management understands the value of a well-organized architecture, they do not know how to achieve it. Therefore, they may make decisions that counteract the architect's efforts. This is not a sign of disloyal management but rather an indication that the architect needs to communicate more clearly or frequently with management. Management must be kept actively involved and informed throughout the process.

- **Culture shock.** Consider how the working culture will change among those who will be affected by the architecture. Try to imagine how easy or difficult it will be for the employees to change their behavior within the organization. People who are flexible and work closely in a dynamic external environment may find it easy to understand new approaches and gain new insights. However, creative environments are no guarantee of a willingness to change. A strong sense of professional identity can be a thick wall to break through. An enterprise architect works extensively with *elaborating how development is achieved* and therefore needs to be in contact with various types of developers and creative minds throughout the organization. Developers are often used to working under unrestricted circumstances, while enterprise architects use formalized tools to coordinate different business improvement initiatives.

- **Inexperienced project leader.** Make sure that the project manager has experience with enterprise architecture. If this is not the case, encourage the sponsor to change the project manager.

Gathering knowledge and getting started

Based on the driving forces behind the EA work, you can determine the areas of business that will be covered by the EA project. Try to find business models that have already been produced. In particular, look into software requirement specification projects, process mapping activities, and reviews of business operations. These may contain a goldmine of models that can be reused. Look also for business model diagrams, preferably on a high level and without too many details that reflect business angles. Try to get access to models that cover the entire business and understand the purpose behind each model, as the reason for creating a model diagram determines how it should be interpreted. Although earlier models may not be entirely up to date, it is possible to discern thoughts, understand structures, and find ideas for designing future process diagrams from the business's previous work.

Look not only at historical materials, but also at operational development currently in progress. It is not unusual for ten development projects to be taking place at the same time and, naturally, for there to be a certain degree of overlap between the projects. These redundancies may be one of the main reasons for adding architecture to the business's agenda. The city plan will provide a clear picture of the overlaps. Research the scope of ongoing initiatives and obtain a view of the participating business representatives. Of course, there may be questions about how resources will be shared between projects.

Look beyond the organization to the external environment in which you are operating. Obtain an overview of what is happening around the enterprise, as well as what is going on upstream and downstream in the business's value chain[1]. If the organization's suppliers or sub-suppliers are implementing or planning for major changes, the city plan should show the impact on the organization of these future plans. The city plan should also indicate if something similar is taking place in regards to the organization's customers. Ongoing standardization processes and future

---

[1] A value chain is a chain of activities that a firm operating in a specific industry performs in order to deliver something valuable (product or service) . (Wikipedia)

legislation are other aspects that can be crucial to the business's working conditions.

Ask to be brought up to date on current internal strategic plans. The clearer these plans are, the easier it will be to understand how the enterprise architecture can affect the business's goals. Try to relate the driving forces behind the city planning process to the applicable goals and strategies. Do not be afraid to contact those who developed the strategies to make sure that you are clear on the strategies' contents. Generally, more has been thought and said than is reflected in strategic documents. This is also a good opportunity to spread the word about the EA concept.

Find out how development is currently progressing, both in business and operational development, as well as in more IT-related processes such as requirements specification, procurement, and implementation. Focus in particular on how development initiatives arise and are initiated.

Conclude the initiation process by gathering together all of the workshop participants, the project manager, and the sponsor for a kick-off event. Address everyone's personal expectations of the process and its expected results. Take this opportunity to promote enthusiasm for enterprise architecture by using simple analogies to illustrate its benefits.

The sponsor should begin his or her talk by emphasizing that the participants have been specially selected to contribute their specialized knowledge, and that management has high expectations of them. The project manager should outline how the work will begin and ensure full participation in planned activities. The enterprise architect should explain how participants will continue working after the first set of results is produced. It is a good idea to conclude the kick-off with listing the key factors for successful EA work.

The above-mentioned activities all affect the order in which EA activities should be conducted and who should be participating in the workshops. Feel free to adapt the EA process described in this book to your individual situation.

Checklist: Results of the initiation

Once the "Initiation" step is complete, you should have the answers to the following questions:

- Why should we do this? The benefits to the business are known, and the process for producing these benefits has been harmonized with current strategic plans.
- Is everybody aware of why EA is being implemented? All necessary people are aware of the major problems, and a plan is in place to enhance awareness, if needed.
- Who is taking responsibility for solving the problem? A strong sponsor has been appointed, along with a senior management team that will participate in the project.
- Who should participate? A correctly staffed project organizational group has been appointed. Participants are invited and are aware of the methods applied in enterprise architecture efforts.
- What are the risks? Risks have been identified and assessed. A plan has been developed to specify how these risks will be handled.
- Are there ongoing parallel activities to consider? Ongoing parallel efforts are known and their influence on the EA project has been defined.
- Are there previous results that we can reuse? Existing useful diagrams are known and available.

Conclude the initiation by compiling the results in a feasibility study report. Present the report to management to obtain a formal decision on the project's continuation.

1.2 MODELING THE BUSINESS PROCESSES AND INFORMATION

Figure 1.4   The EA process method focusing on the first stage, "Ready."

In this section, we will outline how to describe the three elements of a city plan: the business's processes, its information structure, and its supporting systems. We will also outline how to describe the connections between these elements. Furthermore, we will look into how to express the business's expectations. This step includes business innovation modeling, which will influence the target enterprise architecture. Finally, we will discuss an example of how business strategy discussions affect the architecture.

The first stage of the EA process uses models to describe the business areas that are to be covered by the architecture. This provides a map of the processes and business information structure, along with a description of the business objectives, customer values, and key success factors. Work should be conducted in workshops in which valuable knowledge is compiled in a creative manner. As the models produced in the first stage will set the tone for continued EA work, they must be both correct and easy to understand. It is not necessary for them to be extremely detailed in order to serve as the basis for architectural analysis and planning.

Modeling business processes

It is especially important to be prepared for the first workshop, as this is where many of the participants will get their first taste of the EA modeling methods. Spend some time studying existing process diagrams and descriptions and sketch possible process structures in advance. Begin the workshop by allowing the participants to become acquainted with one another and describe the approach that will be followed during the meetings. The graphic design language will be new to many and generally will need explaining. At the same time, keep up the pace during the workshop. The participants' time is valuable and their workloads will increase while they are in attendance.

The first task of the workshop is to determine the scope and level of detail of the process map based on the purpose of the entire architecture effort. Do not allow the map to become too narrow. Extend the process map in both directions along the value chain by starting from early activities in which a real need arises and moving up to the point at which that need is actually met. Because the future architecture should enable the creation of value for the customers and stakeholders of the business, the process map must be extended to include both of these groups.

Together with the participants, express the scope of the process map in concrete terms and determine whether the focus will be on current or future processes. If the focus is on future "to-be" processes, a consensus will be required on the current "as-is" processes. If there are contradicting opinions about "as-is" processes, spend some time describing the processes in general terms. Otherwise, without a common current base, your work on future processes might fail.

Use common process description methods, e.g. moving from left to right, and write down the main activities that make up the business. A good way to produce a map, such as the BestBoatBuilder.com process map in Figure 1.5, is to use the following steps:

www.BestBoatBuilder.com process map - to-be perspective

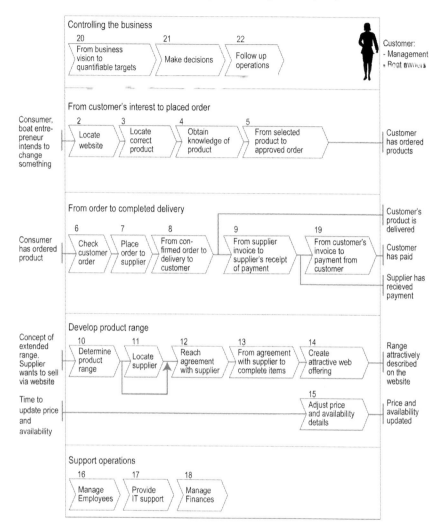

Figure 1.5   Example of a high-level process map containing three end-to-end process chains. Note that the process structure does not reflect the organizational structure or supporting systems.

1. Identify process results and customers (located to the right of the map in Figure 1.5). Strive to have results for external customers in top-level process maps.

2. Identify start events that correspond to the process results (left of the map) and strive to have external process triggers. This way the process map will, in combination with external customer process results, cover "end-to-end processes" rather than being restricted to organizational borders.

3. Identify the major processes in between each start event-result combination. Start from the left of the map. In Figure 1.5, major processes are located inside small boxes.

4. Name the processes with both a verb and a noun, such as "Check customer order" in Figure 1.5.

5. Assign a name for the entire end-to-end flow, such as "Develop product range."

The BestBoatBuilder.com process map in Figure 1.5 is an example of how core processes have been organized in value-creating flows to form end-to-end process chains. Drawing the process map in this manner allows it to reflect the process structure on two levels within one diagram.

Document the processes within the scope of the architecture and structure them so that the map accurately reflects the processes from the perspective of value creation. Separating governing processes and support processes graphically can be beneficial. Usually, the governing processes are placed on the top of the map and the supporting processes on the bottom, as is done in Figure 1.5.

Determine if any processes on the map require further detail. If this is the case, produce more detailed process model diagrams for these processes using the steps given above.

Strive to make the process descriptions as "clean" as possible—that is, make sure that the process diagrams describe the business operations independent of organizational structure, system functions and restrictions, and today's problems.

A process is a series of activities; this is precisely what a process map should describe. Too often, people try to include all aspects of the process in a logical sequence—actors, documents, information flows, and functions. Although it may be easy to reach agreement on such a description, it is not useful for the objective of building an enterprise architecture. In this situation, a clean process map is required because we are going to formulate an ideal architecture that will be based on the processes and how they use information, rather than on today's organization and systems.

Try to look at the processes from the customer's perspective. As mentioned in *RecrEAtion* by Chris Potts, "The customer has the process." Start modeling by deciding which parts of your customer's process(es) you want to appear in—and how. BestBoatBuilder.com has chosen to describe their sales processes *from the customer's interest to their placed order*, an "outside-in" perspective.

Ensure that all processes are documented. It is a good idea to distribute the documentation task among the workshop participants. Give them each a few processes along with a description template that has space for start events, results, and a brief description of the process (see Figure 1.6).

Process	No: 6	Name: Check customer order
Part of	From order to completed devilery.	
Start event	Customer has ordered product.	
Results in	The customer order is ready to be ordered from suppliers.	
Process Customer & Customer Value	BestBoatBuilder customer gets what he/she needs. BestBoatBuilder's suppliers also have the opportunity to fulfill the delivery.	
Process description	Check the customer order to ensure that the various parts of the order match up. Check off with supplier. If incorrect, the customer order can be rectified.	
Described by	Markus Olsson	Oct 5, 2013

Figure 1.6   Example of process documentation.

Modeling the business information structure

In addition to describing the processes, we must also define the business information structure. In fact, the business information structure of an operation is its only truly stable phenomenon. Technology, organization, and working methods are constantly changing. The methods we use today to submit our tax returns, reserve and pay for travel, borrow books from the library, bet on soccer matches, or carry out numerous other everyday actions are completely different from the ways in which we did all of these things ten years ago. However, the business information structure for these examples remains largely unchanged. Its stable properties mean that the business information structure is well suited to be the foundation on which to base a long-term architecture.

Unlike a process model, there is no flow in an information model, no "left to right" or "top to bottom." Instead, the structure is static, which is the characteristic that gives the information model its strength. While processes are constantly being improved, and therefore changed, the information handled by the processes remains the same. For example, even if a sales process is changed dramatically, it still includes *customers* who place *orders* that, in turn, indicate *products*. These business concepts are typical examples that can be modeled, as in Figure 1.7.

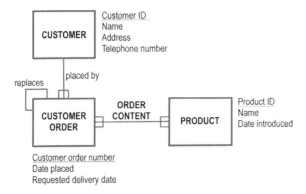

Figure 1.7   Example of a business information model.

Oh no, not data modeling!

When modeling a business information structure, we suggest using a business-oriented data modeling method. Data modeling has been used by IT departments when designing database systems since the seventies. So how is it possible for an analytical exercise as detailed and introspective as data modeling to be of significant use to business representatives? Data modeling often has a bad reputation among business people. "It is what geeks do, just because they are good at it and like it" is one of the most common statements that we hear. Many modern developers decline to use data modeling because they see it as a part of an outdated programming environment. They are interested in other diagrams that are more useful for systems design and programming such as the class diagram in the Unified Modeling Language (UML). Many business representatives have bad experience from data modeling with IT professionals. Business analysts have tried to use data models to explain how the users interact with systems, but this process usually results in an intimidated user and a useless diagram.

Nevertheless, the need for a visual business information structure should be obvious; we cannot describe a business without also describing what kinds of information it uses and produces. Therefore, we do not suggest modeling data by using intimidating graphics. Our guidelines and approach to data modeling makes sure that it is applied in a business-friendly and useable manner. The architectural analysis and the initial architecture design are based on the business information structure, meaning that the business information structure must be modeled in some way. We prefer to call the model of the business information structure a *business information model* to avoid any association with the database design diagrams within the IT department. For those who are already familiar with data modeling, we are talking about a high-level data model that reflects important business concepts.

For forming high-level data models, we refer the reader to other books on this subject, such as *Data Modeling Made Simple* by Steve Hoberman, to gain basic knowledge for this technique. For more advanced modeling techniques, we recommend *Data Modeling for the Business* by Hoberman S., Burbank D., and Bradley C.

Next, we present a brief introduction to business information modeling. For experienced data modelers, this is a selection of what we think are the most important ingredients to use when performing data modeling from a pure business perspective when working with business representatives. However, it is important that experienced data modelers who wish to do business information modeling step outside of their comfort zone of details and data storage design and start working from a business perspective.

Business information modeling basics

When modeling business information, that information is classified into different types according to the different resources and events that occur in the business. The main component in information modeling is the *entity*. An entity is a business concept that has two important aspects: it has uniquely defined occurrences and it is described by its attributes. In the example in Figure 1.7, there are three entities: Customer, Customer Order, and Product. The enterprise architecture's concept of the Customer includes important information that the business has about its customers. There are many customers, each of whom can be easily identified using customer numbers.

Entities are described with *attributes*. An attribute is a business concept that depends on, as well as describes, an entity. In Figure 1.7, there are attributes connected to the Customer entity such as names, addresses, and telephone numbers. The two other entities in Figure 1.7 have identifiers ensuring that their occurrences can be uniquely captured: the Customer Order entity has a Customer Order number, while each Product has a Product ID.

Attributes are grouped with the entities on which they have complete and functional dependence, so that a particular type of fact may only occur once and at the appropriate location in the information model. Using this method of grouping means that all attributes should be located with the entities they describe. Consequently, a product's name is located with the entity Product even though product names occur together with customer orders on order sheets and in data entry forms. Experienced data modelers recognize this way of associating attributes with entities; they call it normalization. For more details on how normalization works, we refer the reader to the titles mentioned previously on this subject.

Entities are bound together by relationships that describe the connection(s) between the entities. In broad terms, there are three types of relationships:

- **Many-to-one (also called one-to-many).** In Figure 1.7, the relationship between the Customer Order entity and the Customer entity is many-to-one. Each customer order is placed by one customer, but one customer can place many orders. Assign the relationship name from the "many" side of the relationship (Customer Order *placed by* Customer).

- **One-to-one.** In Figure 1.7, one customer's order can be replaced by another order from the same customer (possibly due to a change in an order or a correction), resulting in a new version of the original information in the Customer Order entity. Assign the relationship name in any direction.

- **Many-to-many.** In Figure 1.7, a customer's order can include many products, which are included in the Product entity. A product can also be ordered numerous times. Give the relationship a name which is neutral to the relationship direction and is composed of a noun, preferably. Write down many-to-many relationships using uppercase letters, just as you have done with the entities, as sometimes these relationships end up being classified as entities. For example, the Order Contents relationship may end up being the Customer Order Line entity. Though this naming method may seem confusing at first, it is just two ways of expressing business semantics. The main difference between classifying something as an entity versus a relationship at this stage is that an entity is perceived as more important than a relationship.

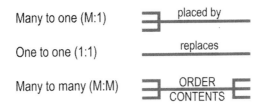

Figure 1.8   Three types of relationships in an information model, with the naming conventions and notation used in this book.

From studying the three types of relationships in Figure 1.8, an experienced data modeler might think, "This is a common logical data model; why suggest a new name?" or, "Why not use a conceptual data model?" The answer is that we need both types of models: we need an enterprise-wide conceptual data model expressed as a logical data model. Logical data models are usually too detailed and focus too narrowly on a project or a system. Conceptual data models are usually not compliant with the normalization rules and do not express the relationships precisely enough. Therefore, we introduce the business information model.

Focus on establishing a relationship line between two entities and decide if each line has a "many" symbol or not. Do not go into extreme detail; otherwise, people will lose interest. In order to begin analyzing and forming the enterprise architecture, it is sufficient to have an overall picture of the important information assets.

How to produce a business information model

Make the information model applicable to the whole enterprise and model it in workshops with business experts. It is preferable to gather the same participants that were in the process map workshop. Begin the information model workshop by listing the most central concepts within the scope of the architecture. If the process map for the enterprise has already been developed, it can be used as a basis for discussions. Identify the key entities in the information model, based either on existing data models or concepts listed during the workshop. Demonstrate the structure between these entities by establishing and naming relationships. Build up the information model one area at a time and involve the workshop group throughout the process.

Use a simple, formal, graphical modeling language with business representatives similar to what we use in this book. If you use more of an IT-focused graphical language, there is a risk that the business participants will have difficulty understanding the syntax and will quickly lose interest. Therefore, use a limited number of symbols so that participants can quickly learn how to interpret the information model. In regards to relationships, the symbols used in Figure 1.8 are ample for working with business representatives.

A business information model contains the most central information entities and the core relationships of the business. The key feature of this model is that the terminology is close to that which is used in the business. Figure 1.9 is an example of an information model of the connection between customer sales and purchasing. Note that the business information structure applies to both semi-manual procedures as well as fully automated procedures such as purchasing via the Internet.

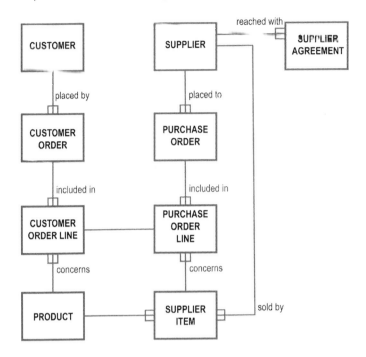

Figure 1.9   BestBoatBuilder.com's example of a business information
               model. The example in Figure 1.7 has been extended with
               entities that reflect purchasing information.

In certain cases, it is necessary to develop more detailed models for each entity (e.g. one for Product, one for Customer, one for Customer Order, etc.). If the city plan you are developing covers a wide area, do not be surprised if the modeling process results in the identification of between 80 and 100 entities.

Prepare for an information modeling workshop by studying earlier models and definitions. If this material is not available within the organization, look at the literature and standard models that are available for review. Use the outcome from the work with the process model workshop to predict the types of business concepts that will arise. Involve the EA project team in the preparation efforts. Advance preparation is especially important if there is more than one facilitator conducting the workshop.

Plan in advance the layout of the model so that the entities end up in the proper spot from the outset. When conducting a workshop, you want to focus more on the participants than on the model's layout.

Reuse existing models and definitions, if available. So that participants can check entity definitions immediately, bring printouts or otherwise ensure that you have access to a library of concepts, if such a repository is available within the enterprise. Having quick access to definitions and earlier models makes the workshop more efficient since time will not be wasted on discussing aspects that have already been established.

Documenting a business information model

Write down a description of each entity in the information model. Give each entity a unique name to be used throughout the enterprise. Where necessary, define any synonyms or abbreviations.

Ensure that the information model is described with the vocabulary used in the business. Significant association with IT terminology could cause discussions to head in the wrong direction and business representatives may, again, lose interest. For this reason, avoid unnecessary detail and focus instead on semantics about core resources and events in the business.

Document the information model both verbally and graphically, as in Figure 1.10. Translate the model into text by explaining it in everyday terms so that it is understandable even by workers who did not participate in the workshop.

The greater the number of people who review and provide feedback on the model, the greater the opportunity to produce a high quality model. Having several people give constructive criticism on the model will help the architecture implementation stages run smoothly.

Graphic information model

Information model described in text

CUSTOMER ORDER `41`

included in

CUSTOMER ORDER LINE `42`

concerns

PRODUCT `3`

A Customer Order contains one or several Lines. One such Customer Order Line refers to a Product. The Customer Order Line can only occur in a single Customer Order.

A Product can occur in several Customer Orders or even multiple times in a single Customer Order.

Figure 1.10   Example of graphical and verbal documentation. This is a detail from entities in Figure 1.9. The number in each entity box is an identifier for the entity to enable traceability if the business decides to change the entity name.

It is a good idea to review process maps, process models, and associated descriptions after the information modeling workshop. Correct the language and names in the models to the previously agreed-upon terminology. Doing this allows the entire set of process materials to become well honed since the precise definitions of the information model are applied to the processes' descriptions.

A successful business information model for EA purposes meets the following criteria:

- The semantics is entirely independent of organizational structures. You should not be able to see the organization in a business information model.
- Definitions are neutral but still relevant for all business processes.

- Definitions are neutral in regards to existing information systems.
- The model reflects how things should be, rather than the as-is situation.
- The model should have stringency and be unambiguous. It should only be able to be interpreted in one way.
- The model covers the entire scope of your city plan.

Once these conditions have been met, the structure is sustainable enough to form the basis of a long-term architecture.

The order of the activities in the EA process can vary greatly depending on what is going on in the business when the EA initiative starts. We suggest modeling the business processes before the business information. A process model is easier for business representatives to understand and discuss, and it is slightly easier to model business processes than it is to model information. By beginning with processes, participants become accustomed to the modeling method and will be better prepared for creating a picture of the information structure, which is somewhat harder to interpret for most people.

Expressing business expectations

In a global and continuously changing world in which business operations and IT are strongly intertwined, flexibility and future-proof investments are of significant value to every company. A well-organized enterprise architecture is a foundation for efficient and profitable business operations. It is therefore crucial that the enterprise architect becomes acquainted with the company's business rules and actively cooperates with business developers and managers. The architect's overarching objective is to maximize business benefits in the long term for both the company and its customers.

It is increasingly crucial for companies to be able to continually question and improve the business strategies of their organizations. Previously, companies were characterized by a single dominant way of earning money. Their strategy for gaining a competitive advantage primarily entailed enhancing process efficiency and optimizing the organization accordingly, along with improving production speed and capacity. Now, with other companies in the sector taking the same approach, relying on one profit generating method will result in a downward spiral of price pressure, shrinking margins, and, in the end, impaired profitability. Naturally, efficiency enhancement and product development remain central ingredients, but such a strategy is not, by itself, sufficient for a company's long-term survival.

Today, companies operate in sectors characterized by multiple, coexisting ways of doing business, which often compete against one another. In the aviation industry, for example, there are traditional operators, low-cost airlines, airlines solely for business travel, and private jet operators. Each operator's way of doing business emphasizes unique customer values and offers different attributes as incentives. For companies to be able to ensure that their development is strategically sustainable, they must work purposefully to innovate how customer value is created, to communicate their uniqueness, and to continuously improve their business. Essentially, they must stand out from the crowd.

As a consequence of the increasing pace and number of competitors, it is not enough to provide only the right offerings with the right attributes. Demands for cost efficiency also mean that we need to develop and optimize our network of partners and generate value where it can be achieved most efficiently. The classic sequential value chain is being discarded, and instead networks and loosely coupled partnerships that generate results through interaction and an increasing degree of synchronicity are being established. The global supply of services and goods, as well as the Internet and automated services, are generating new opportunities for cooperation between organizations and countries in ways that were not possible in the past. People and companies are now interacting and competing with one another in a global market.

Expressing business expectations using Osterwalder's Business Model Canvas

A Business Model Canvas shows how an organization intends to earn money by generating and delivering value. It describes what the company offers its customers; how that offering reaches the customers; through what resources, activities, and partners the company creates its offering; and, finally, the sustainability and profitability of the business.

Until recently, a company's method of innovation was unique to each enterprise and usually ended up looking like an unstructured and disorganized process. It is very hard for an enterprise architect to work with such a mysterious business model. Using a Business Model Canvas, business innovation can become a structured process with clear results that the whole organization can understand and build upon.

Alexander Osterwalder, the inventor of the Business Model Canvas concept, visualizes a business by describing these nine building blocks (see Figure 1.11):

- **Customer Segments**. Charting customer groups and the actions that generate true benefits for customers.
- **Value Propositions**. The combination of services and products that generate value for our customers.
- **Channels**. The channels through which we communicate with our customers and advertise our offerings.
- **Customer Relationships**. The ways in which we establish and maintain relations with our customers.

- **Revenue Streams**. The revenue flows generated from our customers.
- **Key Resources**. The principal resources on which we build our business.
- **Key Activities**. The key activities that must be carried out to generate the customer value.
- **Key Partners**. The partners and suppliers with whom we work.
- **Cost Structure**. The costs incurred in creating and running the business.

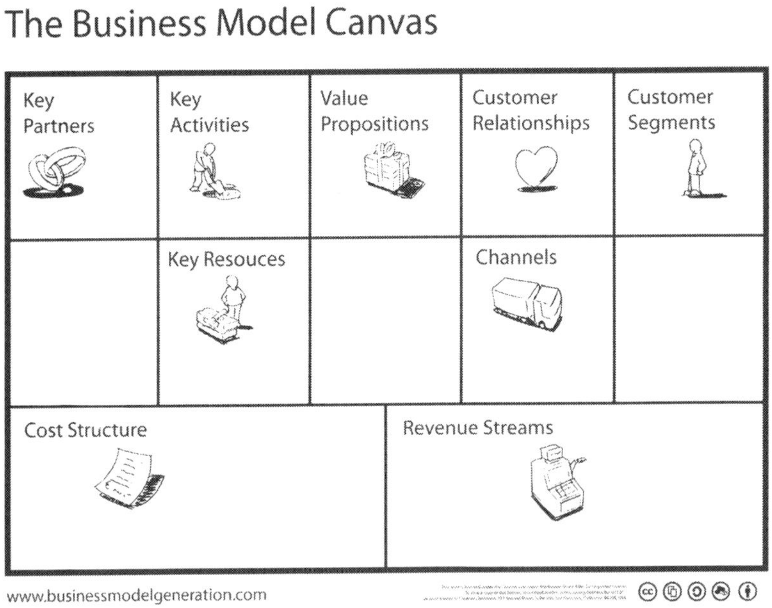

The Business Model Canvas

Key Partners	Key Activities	Value Propositions	Customer Relationships	Customer Segments
	Key Resouces		Channels	
Cost Structure		Revenue Streams		

Figure 1.11 The Osterwalder Business Model Canvas. © Alexander Osterwalder. Used with permission.

There is a wealth of different ways to describe how a business is conducted, and the Business Models Canvas is one of these methods. This type of model is easily understood by managers and business developers and is therefore an excellent bridge of communication between the IT and business fields for the enterprise architect. Changes in the Business Models Canvas give rise to the development of both processes and systems, while the business information structure may remain relatively unaffected.

Cooperate with business innovators by introducing them to the Business Model Canvas (if they are not using the tool already). Assisting the Innovators with modeling the business canvas will give you valuable insight about how the business will be formed, or at least how it is expected to be formed. The business innovators may find the city plan models to be of great use, and they should be introduced to them as well.

Be aware of name confusion. For an enterprise architect, a business model is probably a diagram illustrating a business structure, such as a process map. For most business representatives, a business model illustrates how the enterprise earns its money and attracts customers. Be sure to label your diagrams properly.

Expressing business expectations using Ross's Operating Model

Discussing the value of the customers and the processes is not an easy task. Just showing a newly modeled process map and the latest version of a strategy document may lead to a constrained discussion. To widen the scope of the discussion, propose a new approach or idea and use it as a tool to discuss your business from a different mindset. The Business Model Canvas and the Operating Model are two such tools.

In the article *Forget Strategy: Focus IT on Your Operating Model*, Jeanne W. Ross of MIT describes how to position the business from another perspective. Her operating model (Figure 1.12) can be used to discuss and determine how the company's process structure is established at the moment and how it should be changed in the future.

Four operating models

Figure 1.12   Ross's Four Operating Models. © Jeanne Ross. Used with permission.

By combining only two dimensions, the standardization and the integration of your business processes, the four quadrants in the operating model each describe a direction for how to form business operations. Consequently, each quadrant also indicates directions for the enterprise architecture.

- **Coordination.** Low standardization and high integration. Business units do not use the same processes because they perform different kinds of services. However, they may address the same customer and need to be aware of what other units are doing. Business information is shared across the units.

- **Replication.** This is the opposite of coordination and involves high standardization and low integration. Processes are similar or identical, and all customers are experiencing the same value and treatment. Business units likely are not aware of the total engagement of individual customers.

- **Unification**. High standardization and high integration. Processes are similar and transparency between processes is complete. A customer can do business with any business unit and receive the same kind of service.

- **Diversification**. This is the opposite of unification and is characterized by low standardization and low integration. Business units function independently of one another, often because they are working in completely different lines of business. They may be competing on the same market, such as having different brands with a common owner.

The degree of standardization and integration between processes affects the architecture to a noticeable degree and is therefore of great interest to the enterprise architect. How do these quadrants guide the design of the enterprise architecture? Wherever there is process that needs to be standardized, it is a challenge to determine the ideal standardization level. While some processes may be "common processes," others may be "identical processes." Identical processes may use the same configuration of IT-systems support and commonly need local independence.

Process integration implies that business information definitions are standardized. Process integration is not only about sharing information, but also about understanding shared information. A coordinated or unified operating model needs an information-centric enterprise architect. Most enterprise architects strive for process standardization by working towards a common system landscape throughout the enterprise.

A diversified operating model does not need a common architecture. Apart from financial reporting at the group level, it is unnecessary for it to have common enterprise architecture. However, in allowing the enterprise architects to learn from each other, they can collaborate on determining the best practices in EA for working methods, communication, tools, etc.

It is less necessary for a company with low demands on integration and standardization of processes to form a city plan encompassing the entire enterprise than it is for an organization that needs to integrate and standardize a large number of processes. For the latter, it is crucial to take the entire business into account when forming the city plan.

For deeper insight about Ross' operating model, we refer to *Enterprise Architecture as Strategy: Creating a Foundation for Business Execution*, by W. Ross, J., Weil, P., C. Robertson, D.

Weighing the standardization and integration of processes requires the active involvement of management. The operating model is useful in discussing architecture with management. By determining the enterprise's position in the model, you can clarify the collective demands placed on the capacities of both processes and systems.

Linking business processes to objectives and values

Study the strategies and business objectives of the enterprise and determine the expectations of the different business areas as expressed through initiative directives, business concepts, growth targets, and similar steering documents. Revisit the driving force behind the EA assignment and make a list of the main challenges currently facing the business.

Attempt to identify the processes that affect these objectives from the process map. Make comments about how processes influence the business in regards to overcoming particular challenges and examine possible contradictions in the combination of processes and objectives. Such an analysis provides insight into future process development and, ultimately, the possible effects on the final architecture.

Determine which key success factors should be applied by the business in order for them to be able to meet their objectives within the scope of the processes. In particular, try to indicate which success factors apply to which processes. In the BestBoatBuilder.com example, supplying the right order items is vital for customer satisfaction. Therefore, having someone check each customer's order in the "Check customer order" process is a success factor for making sure that a customer is buying the items she or he really needs.

Identify customers and results for the end-to-end process. Start a discussion, preferably within the strategy group of the EA assignment, about which customer values the business should focus on fulfilling. Express both rational customer values, such as price, availability, and product quality, and emotional customer values, such as brand value and the prestige followed by having the product. Give these values a priority rank so that you can decide which values that should be fulfilled first. Indicate the processes in which customer value is added.

Identify your strategically important processes. They need special attention in your EA. Strategically important processes are those that make the business unique. It is because of these processes that there are customers who choose to buy from your organization and keep coming back. Unique processes allow the organization to become a market leader and stand out from its competition.

A strategic process may include business secrets, which means that it must be kept secure to prevent competitors and customers from gaining access to it. Check if the strategically important processes have experienced problems previously, are currently working incorrectly or inefficiently, or are expected to face problems in the future.

It is not always possible for representatives from all parts of a large global organization to meet with one another in order to discuss the future structure of the enterprise. One approach to coordinating members of a global company is to build the city plan gradually. While positioning one's business in the model, consider whether it is necessary to deal with the entire company at one time. The greater the need for integration, the wider the scope of what is included in the architecture process. If there is a significant need for integration, most or all of the business's processes must be included in the city plan.

Involve senior management when determining what operating model to strive for and how it will impact your target enterprise architecture. Let the EA project strategy group discuss this issue in one of the executive management meetings. The discussion by executives is beneficial not only for improving the quality of the architecture, but also because it brings enterprise architecture to the top floor of your organization.

Well-prepared meetings with members of management are necessary for them to understand the Business Model Canvas, along with the business's objectives, prioritized customer values, success factors, strategic processes, and the degrees of integration and standardization between processes. Plan more than one meeting and allow time between them for the participants to evaluate and reconsider their answers to the questions that arise.

Our example company, BestBoatBuilder.com, has decided to use the Replication Operational Model. In this type of model (shown in Figure 1.13), the same lineup of processes applies to any country the company enters. Two processes are considered strategically important: *Locate website* and *From selected product to approved order*.

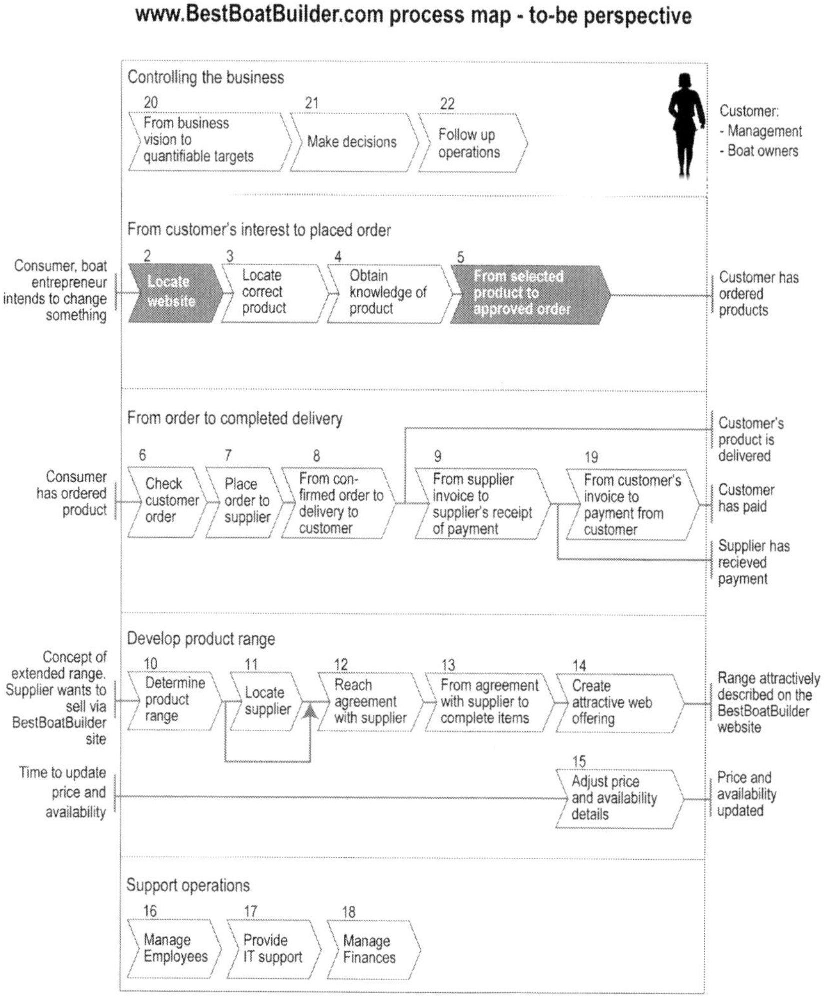

www.BestBoatBuilder.com process map - to-be perspective

Figure 1.13   Strategically important processes are emphasized.

1.3 ANALYZING CONSEQUENCES AND OPPORTUNITIES

With the help of the process map and information model, it is possible to evaluate the consequences of the business's current situation and to identify opportunities that the improved architecture can provide. We do this by comparing the information needs of each process with the information that the collective systems portfolio is able to deliver. However, simply examining processes and systems would be an inadequate architectural analysis. Processes cannot be connected to systems without having access to both the information that the process uses and the information that the systems handle. Therefore, models of both processes and information are needed. These models are connected to the systems, as illustrated below in Figure 1.14. Most importantly, business expectations are addressed to business processes and business information, which, in turn, addresses requirements to the systems portfolio.

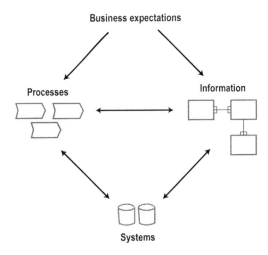

Figure 1.14   Relationships between process, information, and systems.

As the word "architecture" indicates, each individual process, entity, and system should not be considered in isolation. This would make the focus of the architecture far too narrow to be of much use to anyone. Instead, an overall perspective of information requirements and availability is needed. The architectural analysis then involves comparing these views and identifying which information needs are fulfilled and which ones require more attention. In this section, we show how it is possible to derive the business's costs from this analysis. The obvious difference between the information that is needed and the information that is currently available generates significant opportunities for improvement in business development, operations, and IT.

Identifying entity groups

Start by making the information models easier to understand for everyone working on the EA project. The information models produced earlier in the EA process can be difficult to interpret for those not involved in the modelling process. Normally, only the modelers and IT architects are able to understand what the models are saying with a minimum of background explanation. Therefore, you need to establish a manageable number of entity groups. Between 30 and 50 is by experience a manageable amount. A too large a number of entity groups will make the EA analysis and design too complex.

An entity group, sometimes known as a subject area, contains one or more entities along with their associated relationships, which together form a logical, coherent component. Figure 1.15 shows how sixteen model elements (six entities and five relationships with a symbol at either end) have been reduced to four entity groups representing important business concepts.

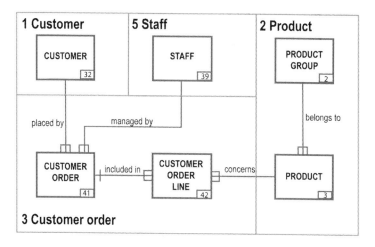

Figure 1.15   Reducing complexity by organizing entities into entity groups.

There is often a "strong" entity that forms the basis of the group (in entity group number 2 (Product) in Figure 1.15, it is the Product entity that forms the basis of this group). Since a strong major entity may be the foundation of an entity group, it is a good idea to give the entity group the same name as its major entity. This naming method dramatically improves clarity and makes communication easier because you can focus on entity groups as a whole, rather than trying to remember which entities make up which entity group. If you hide the entities and relationships by listing only the name of the entity groups, the models look simpler and become easier to understand for those who are not familiar with information modeling. Figure 1.15 is a subset from the entire Entity Group model, as shown in Figure 1.18.

The entity groups build the foundation for your future architecture. Instead of working with over a hundred entities, you only need to have an overall business information model containing a manageable amount of elements reflecting the business's major information assets.

Forming entity groups is quite simple. Make a print-out of the entire information model and mark the border for each entity group clearly, as in the information model in Figure 1.15.

Good grouping follows the principles for normalization and starts with the core entities in the model, which are those of most value to the business. Do not start the modeling process by grouping entities according to their organization, processes, geography, products, or systems since these categories are not stable over time. Be cautious when putting entities in the same group; for example, it is a bad idea to let Purchase Order, Customer Order, and Work Order form an entity group called Order. Even if these entities may appear as similar events, such a generalization may lead the architecture analysis in the wrong direction since they have very different life cycles. It will also be difficult to find someone willing to take responsibility for such a generalized entity group.

Be particularly careful when making groupings for M:M (many-to-many) relationships. A simple rule is that M:M relationships belong to the same entity group as the entity emerging last in the relationship. In Figure 1.16, the Order Content relationship ends up in the same entity group as the entity Purchase order, since a Purchase Order and its Order Contents can be created when information on Supplier items is already available.

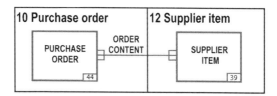

Figure 1.16   Grouping of many-to-many relationships.

Give each entity group a name and number as well as a short verbal description. Assign the entity groups to a separate number series other than the series for the entities it contains.

Determining information life cycle type

By now, all major entities within the domain of the city plan are modeled and arranged into entity groups. Before finalizing your results from the information modeling process, you need to look at the overall picture of the entity groups. One way of doing this is to look at each entity's lifecycle, growth, and information usage, as described below.

Based on the lifecycle of information, there are four distinguishable basic information types:

- Category information
- Resource information
- Business event information
- Detail operational transaction information

This classification is vital to the planning of architecture work since different types of information require different approaches, as shown in the table in Figure 1.17. Entities should therefore be classified according to these information types by an experienced information modeler.

Information types	Characteristics			
	Entity examples	Volume	Growth	Architecture goal
Category	Market Product Group Customer Type Mode of Delivery	Few values	None	Business monitoring using standardized values
Resource "Master Data"	Product Personnel Customer	Many	Follows the size of the organization and business volume	High data quality by standardized definitions and appointed sources
Business Event "Business Data"	Sales Order Delivery event Payment	Very many	Follows (is) the business volume	Efficient business by standard definitions suitable for daily operations
Detail Operational Transaction "Big data"	An interrupted phone call Vehicle log Geographical movement	Vast	Growth increases with the business volume	Enable "big data" to become useful knowledge by putting it into appropriate contexts

Figure 1.17   Characteristics of four types of information that correspond to the lifecycle of the entities.

Category information

Categories provide a way to classify each entity occurrence or record based on similar characteristics. For example, if there are thousands of customers, the business will probably want to look at the ones that are in similar market categories or business sectors and which have the same method of contact, product type, media type, etc. Categories that are used across the organization usually form their own entities. A category entity provides one set of alternatives by which something may be classified. Generally, it has few occurrences and a hierarchic structure. An entity occurrence may be classified in many ways, so there can be many category entities in a model. For example, the products could be classified by fuel, color, model, etc. It is a good idea to ensure that the aspect forming the category is applicable across the entire business.

It can be difficult to standardize category entities because they have no active lifecycle. Unlike other types of information, categories usually contain information that is fairly static and has no natural source within business operations. At the same time, it is normally on the basis of the categories that the business determines the parts of the company that it should focus on improving first—deciding which Customer groups, Markets, and Product areas will receive special attention, for example. Consequently, standardizing key category occurrences may require the architect to work closely with senior management. Category entities seldom form their own entity groups and, in fact, generally belong in the group with the entity that they are categorizing.

Resource information

As the name suggests, *resource information* symbolizes information based on the basic resources that are required to conduct an operational process such as Product, Customer, Supplier, Facility, Organization, and Staff. These are classical entities that are used throughout the enterprise. Good architecture entails maintaining the high information quality of a resource entity through centralized quality assurance and shared use of the data. This can be achieved by using master data solutions such as central databases or master data hubs. A resource entity often has many occurrences (records or rows) and generally grows with the size of the business. Your process map should have processes that secure and maintain your core resource identities.

Resource entities usually need most attention by the enterprise architects. Therefore, resource information is divided into four types: organizational, external parties, infrastructure, and product. This is discussed in the next session.

Business event information

Business event information is generated while operational processes are in progress. Business event entities are often established so that processes can be kept together. Major business events form entities such as Customer Orders, Supplier Invoices, Cash Withdrawal, and Business Meetings. Among IT professionals, event entities are sometimes referred to as transactional business data.

The impact of an event entity varies in accordance with the business being modeled. The number of entity occurrences often grows constantly. Event data are generally captured, used, and deleted locally. It is not always necessary to see the details of all event data. It is uncommon, for example, for management to want to know how many buns a particular customer bought at a certain bakery on Friday, February 4th at 8:33 A.M. On the other hand, it is desirable to aggregate event data to discern totals, deviations, and trends. For this reason, the definition and structure of shared event data should be standardized and made available throughout the business so that information can be compared and understood at different places and areas of operation. Large organizations often put significant resources into establishing a uniform definition of the Customer concept. In the same way, efforts should also be made to define the Customer Contact Event entity.

Business event information is often subject for automation in order to make business processes more efficient. The architecture's challenge is to make sure that the event information is coherent with the overall picture, i.e. that the event entities can relate to other entities in the overall information structure.

Detail operational transaction information ("big data")

"Big data" has become a popular topic over the last few years. It has revealed the level of information management maturity in many organizations as many companies have started to collect great volumes of detailed data. *Detailed operational transaction information* is often produced by sensors in machines, which can be parts of vessels and vehicles, industrial components, or personal devices that we use daily. Transaction information may also be produced by humans through social media systems and other contexts in which we leave electronic footprints as we interact over the Internet.

This type of detailed information is also used for aggregation, deviations, and trends, similar to how the business information events are used. In fact, big data also includes information about events—just much more detailed than the ones listed above. Detailed transaction information is also used for forming structures and principles for simulations since there is enough data to try to produce statistic expressions such as probabilities and correlations. Many companies have formed customized offerings based on customer behavior and newly discovered opportunities for profits.

So what is the challenge here for the enterprise architect? Do not put this information type aside simply because the data is vast and technically oriented. Model it and make room for the big data in the enterprise business information model, at least in a summarized way. That way it will be related and put into the city plan just like any other kind of information. The real challenge for the enterprise architect is to make an understandable and useful picture out of large data sets. As an expert on the value of business information, an enterprise architect can help to accomplish this difficult task.

Distinguishing between resource and event entity groups

The BestBoatBuilder.com example in Figure 1.18 shows the complete, stripped-down picture of its business, with all entity groups defined. The entity groups that deal with business events are colored white and are placed in the center of the model, while those that deal with resource information are gray and placed along the edges.

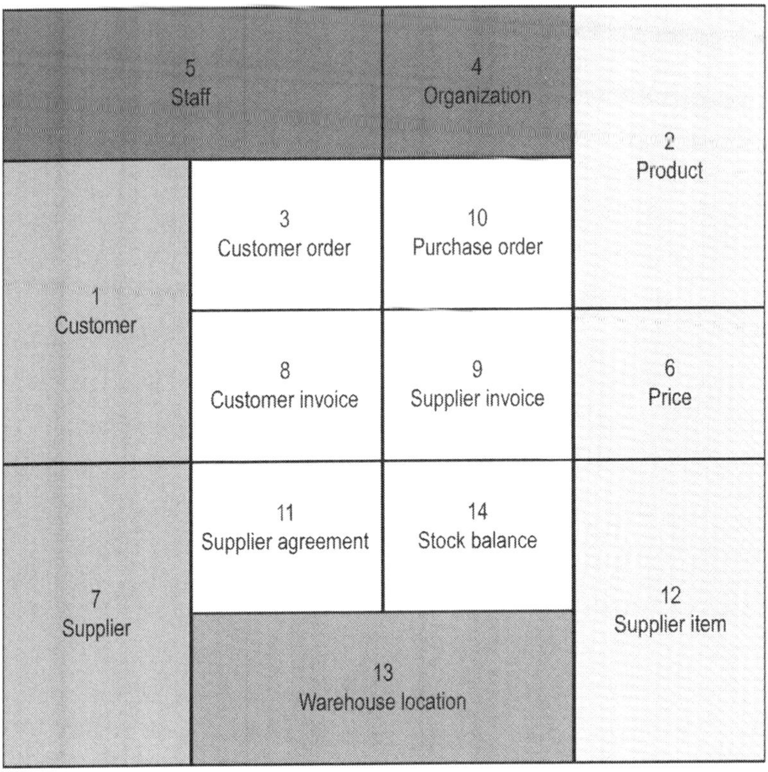

5 Staff	4 Organization	2 Product
1 Customer	3 Customer order	10 Purchase order
	8 Customer invoice	9 Supplier invoice
7 Supplier	11 Supplier agreement	14 Stock balance
	13 Warehouse location	12 Supplier item

Figure 1.18   All entity groups in the BestBoatBuilder.com example. Events are in the middle and resources are at the edges. Entities contained in the entity groups are concealed.

From experience, we know that resource entities need the greatest amount of attention in enterprise architecture work. Category entities take a long time to be established but do not need daily attention. Business events and detailed transactions are usually easy to deal within the project as long as an enterprise architect ensures that they work well together. The resource information entities usually contain the majority of the problems. Therefore, we suggest dividing the resource information category into four sub-types:

- **Product and offering**. Indicates entity groups that contain resource information for products and offerings. In Figure 1.18, the Product (2), Price (6) and Supplier Item (12) entity groups in the BestBoatBuilder.com are examples of this type of resource group.

- **Proprietary resources.** Indicates entity groups containing proprietary resource information on staff, competence, and the organization itself. Financial concepts may be included here. The Staff (5) and Organization (4) entity groups are two such examples.

- **External information.** Denotes entity groups containing information about resources that exist outside of the organization. For example, Customer and Supplier companies exist whether or not they do business with your organization, and legislation and industry standards are created regardless of the actions of your organization. The Customer (1) and Supplier (7) entity groups go in this category.

- **Infrastructure.** Entity groups that reflect physical places and infrastructure. The Warehouse location entity group (13) goes in this category.

Dividing resource entities into different groups and color-coding them to indicate the type of information handled by each group is useful for model management and makes the models easier to understand. Consequently, the business's information can be roughly divided into separate areas that are the same for different companies within the same industry. At this macro level, as in Figure 1.18, many enterprises may appear to be almost identical. An enterprise's uniqueness can be shown through the names and combinations of its entity groups. This is especially the case when examining connections among its business event entity groups, which are the places where the business's value is usually created. Furthermore, customer service businesses tend to have a greater number of event entities, manufacturers must put extensive resources towards building and maintaining physical structures, and pharmaceutical companies have more entities in the product area.

Figure 1.19 illustrates a proposed layout standard for information models. If all information models adhere to the same standard, they will be easier to read and it will be easier to place entities in the appropriate places during modeling workshops. Model management, model content comprehension, the reuse of models, and the quality of the content will improve if all information models follow such a standard.

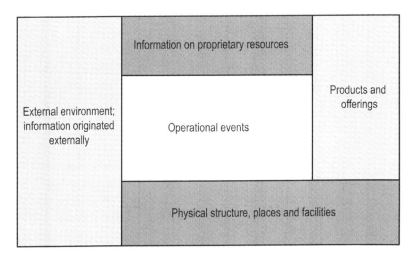

Figure 1.19   Proposed layout standard for entity group models and detailed business information models. Event entities are placed in the middle, and the different types of resource entities are placed along the border.

Note that an entity can be a *resource entity* in one company while being an *event entity* in another. In a trading company, for example, the Product entity is often a resource entity, while in a company that develops (but never manufactures or delivers) new electronics products, the Product entity is classified as an event entity. When deciding how an entity should be classified, avoid considering entities from a process perspective and keep the entire breadth of the business in mind.

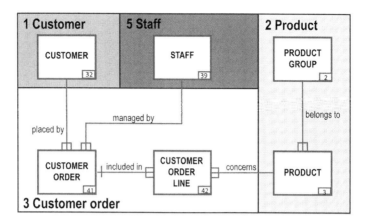

Figure 1.20   An information model with visible entity groups. The figure shows the same model as Figure 1.15 laid out according to the standard.

An entity group should not contain both a core resource entity and a core business event entity. Core resource and core event entities have different types of dependencies and, if mixed together, would give rise to incorrect architecture and plans. To avoid this problem, conduct a review of the grouped entities to ensure that no mix-ups have occurred. Less important event entities, such as a new version of the description of Product, may appear in a resource entity group. As mentioned previously, category entities should not form their own entity groups. Instead, they will probably belong to entity groups for either resource or event entities.

This rule is not fool-proof and it is always necessary to consider each entity individually. If, for example, Supplier is a resource entity and forms an entity group, it is not obvious whether Supplier Agreement is an entity *within* that group or if it belongs in *its own* entity group. In such cases, look at the business rules for the Supplier Agreement. If it is a one-time activity (i.e. it is necessary to have an agreement to become a Supplier, but once that has been secured, the agreement applies for an extended period of continued operations), the Supplier Agreement is presumably an entity in the Supplier entity group. Alternatively, if it is an event that repeats as soon as conditions such as prices for raw materials change, the Supplier Agreement should be in an event entity group called Pricing or should form an entity group of its own.

Describing the processes' need of information

By establishing a process and entity group matrix (or simply a process matrix), one can obtain a clear overview of the information acquired and used in the processes. This matrix should use clear and simple symbols such as the following:

● **Create**: Also includes reading, changing, and removing individual entity occurrences.

○ **Read**: Reads one entity occurrence at a time or a compilation of several occurrences.

⊙ **Change**: Entails changing one entity occurrence at a time as well as reading individual occurrences. This symbol is used infrequently in EA since it would include too much detail. It is however more often used when detailing requirements on specific software.

⊗ **Remove**: Also includes reading; is also uncommon in EA due to same reasons as above.

Fill in the process and entity group matrix in a workshop forum or in working groups. The groups should be comprised of the same people that are involved in developing the process map and the information models. Create a matrix with the processes on the Y-axis. Place the processes by line in the same order as in the process map—that is, in the order in which they normally occur. Place the entity groups by column, preferably grouped in areas similar to the entity group model (see Figure 1.19).

Work with one process at a time. Decide what information (entity group) is needed to be able to perform the process. Mark all such entity groups with an empty ring (O). Mark with a filled ring (●) the entity groups in which new occurrences of the entity arise. In Figure 1.21, the process "From selected product to approved order" has an empty ring (O) in the entity groups Product and Price and a filled ring (●) in the entity groups Customer and Customer Order. The implication is that the process "From selected product to approved order" captures new Customers and Customer Orders and (re-)uses information about Product and Price.

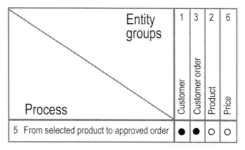

Figure 1.21   A process captures and reuses information.

Do not confuse the process matrix with process input/output. The process matrix also reflects the kind of information that is used within the processes. Business process "input/output" relates only to the interface with other processes and is often document- or systems-oriented.

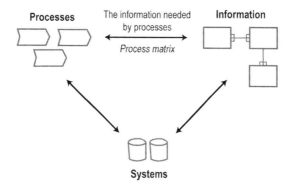

Figure 1.22   The process matrix clarifies information needs.

The process matrix captures much more than this; it provides information that is used within the process and is presumed to be available. By means of the matrix, the process description regarding information needs is clarified significantly.

Fill in the matrix on the premise that each process is isolated. Do not assume that there are connections between the processes even though they may, for example, use the same systems or be performed by the same people.

Processes / Entity groups	1 Customer	2 Customer Order	3 Product	6 Price	8 Customer Invoice	5 Staff	7 Supplier	9 Supplier Invoice	10 Purchase Order	11 Supplier Agreement	23 Supplier Item	13 Warehouse Location	14 Stock Balance
1 Market Offering	O	O		O		O	O						
2 Locate website		O					O			O			
3 Locate correct product			O	O		O	O			O			
4 Obtain knowledge of product			O	O		O	O			O			
5 From Selected Product to Approved Order	●	●	O	O									●
6 Check Customer Order	O	◉	O	O	O	O	O			O	O		O
7 Place Order to Supplier	O	◉				O	O		●	O	O		
8 From Confirmed Order to Delivery to Customer	O	O	O	O		O	O		O	O	O	O	O
9 From Supplier Invoice to Paid Delivery	O	O	O	O	O	O		●	O	O	O		
19 From Customer Invoice to Payment from Customer	O	O	O	O	●	O	O	O					

Figure 1.23 Process matrix example for the BestBoatbuilder.com. The processes are derived from the process map in Figure 1.5. Note the proportions of filled and unfilled rings.

Now connect the use of information to business objectives and customer values. The processes considered to be of strategic importance for the organization were identified previously by linking them to business objectives and customer values. The process matrix now shows which entity groups these processes manage—mainly the types of data that the processes capture and read. Conduct a special overview of these entity groups to check that they are adequately described. Ascertain the form in which these data are needed and how up-to-date they need to be for the strategically important processes to function satisfactorily. This analysis provides two important insights: determining which information is strategic and analyzing how the strategically important processes depend on various other processes.

Describing existing systems

As mentioned previously, processes should be described neutrally in relation to documents, systems, and organization. In fact, in purely logical terms, operational processes cannot be directly linked to systems. The connection between processes and systems occurs, or should occur, via information. To provide a better understanding of the information connection, a system matrix can be constructed. This matrix does not need to go into extreme detail, as a general overview is sufficient enough to generate insights and assess benefit (see Figure 1.24).

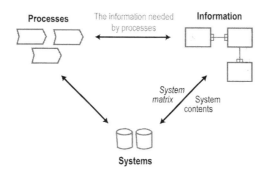

Figure 1.24   The Systems matrix clarifies the contents of the system.

Start by establishing a list of the business systems together with systems managers or other systems experts. Produce a brief description of each system. The description should include systems owners, the technical platform, supplier, age, planned lifecycle, number of users, organizational units or sites that use the system, etc. It can be difficult to define what is meant by "system." In such cases, simplify the definition by, for example, letting one database define one system. Sometimes, several systems may use the same database. In this case, allow all of these databases to be considered together as one system. Include future systems and ongoing projects in this list of descriptions.

Fill in a systems and entity group matrix (or systems matrix) to show which entity groups capture new occurrences (●). Mark with an empty ring (O) where a system reuses/reads entity occurrences captured in another system. Take one system at a time and describe its information contents. Use a filled ring when key information is manually entered into the system. See Figure 1.25.

Systems / Entity Groups	1 Customer	2 Product	3 Customer Order	4 Organization	5 Staff	6 Price	7 Supplier	8 Customer Invoice	9 Supplier Invoice	10 Purchase Order	11 Supplier Agreement	12 Supplier Item	13 Warehouse Location	14 Stock Balance
1 Webshop incl. admin	●	●	●			●	●	○	●					
2 SPDS	●	●	●	●	●	●	●	●	●	●		●		
4 Outlook & Lookout Module	○	●	●		●					●				
6 Watif DirectResponse		●	●			●				●		●	●	●
7 Boatstore DirectResponse		●	●			●				●		●	●	●
8 Rudder Web Shop		●	●			●		●		●		●	●	●
9 Captain Husberg's Internet Store		●	●			●				●		●	●	●
10 BHL Multishipping			●					●		●				
11 Kon-Tiki Sails		●										●	●	●
12 Kybernetes		●												
13 Resource Internet Banking	●				●									
14 Asping Portal		●				●	●					●	●	●

Figure 1.25   Example of a systems matrix.

Note that the systems matrix is not intended to describe data distribution or integration. If two systems supply data to several different systems, both dots and rings are shown. This matrix does not display the senders or recipients of data.

Where necessary, use a special matrix for processes and systems to establish which processes each system supports. Often, these connections can be derived from the other matrices, although a special matrix is sometimes needed to provide insights on how widely certain systems are used. It may also be necessary to delineate which systems are local (such those that are used only in certain countries, or do not contain enterprise-common data), as opposed to the central or enterprise-wide systems, or to divide the systems used for specific product areas into corresponding groups. See Figure 1.26.

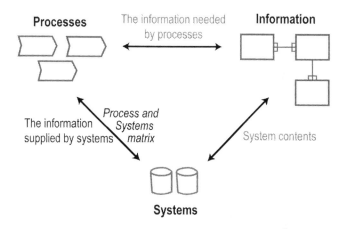

Figure 1.26   Occasionally, a process and systems matrix is also needed. This is more often requested when redesigning processes rather than in EA planning.

Analyzing opportunities and assessing benefit

The knowledge collected so far about the enterprise architecture usually gives insights about the total business situation. A process and entity matrix now exists that has, most likely, 70-80 percent empty rings, with the remainder of rings being filled. It is common for processes to reuse close to 80 percent of existing information that has already been captured in some part of the organization. In the best-case scenario, it is simply a matter of accessing a system, collecting what is needed, and trusting that the information comes from a secure source.

The systems and entity group matrix usually has the inverse proportions; that is, 80 percent of the rings are filled. This means that the same information is entered in several systems independently of one another. Add up the number of filled rings per entity group and identify which have the most. If, for example, there are ten Customer registers, there are potentially ten sets of details for the same Customer. It would be ideal to capture a Customer's details just once, at the source, and to then disseminate the information where it is needed. Consequently, a systems and entity group matrix with 80 percent of its rings filled means that there are considerable opportunities for improvement.

The benefits of architectural improvement can be assessed by examining three perspectives and taking note of how each experiences the benefits relative to one another. These perspectives are:

- Effects in terms of IT (1)
- Effects within the in-house operations (10)
- Effects on customers, partners, and others in the external environment (100).

In our experience, the business operational effects are ten times greater than the IT effects; the effects on the external environment are ten times greater again. See Figure 1.27.

By exercising IT control on the basis of business-based architecture, IT is perceived to be more efficient. Matrices nearly always show that an organization has too many systems and that certain systems are performing the same functions. Consequently, it is easy to derive benefits in the form of, among other things, lower license costs, fewer platforms to maintain, reduced maintenance costs, and lower costs for integration.

However, motivating an EA venture solely on the grounds of reduced IT costs is seldom successful. In part, the benefits to the business from undertaking such a venture are uncertain, since new costs may arise before there has been time to implement an architecture plan, and because, in part, EA requires a great deal of perseverance. Furthermore, the gains derived from more efficient IT are not usually significant. Some claim that the effect on IT does not exceed the cost of the architecture venture. For this reason, presentations about EA implementation should place more emphasis on the numerous benefits to in-house operations and the external environment than on how much EA will lower IT costs.

1. IT	2. Business operation	3. Customer
Only the "right" systems – decreased costs for storage, maintenance, licenses, integration, etc. Faster and more accurate capture of business requirements Increased level of service towards business Easier to live up to process changes	Decreased replication of data entry work Decreased unnecessary work in correcting errors Increased security as a consequence of enhanced data quality Fewer unnecessary telephone calls and meetings Efficient work with proper IT systems Well-being at work Shorter training period for new staff	Less lost business Increased customer loyalty Correct deliveries, on time, to the right address Enhanced customer service and quality experiences Goodwill

Figure 1.27   Examples of benefits.

Consequently, trying to motivate architecture on the sole basis of IT benefit is not sustainable.

If, for example, there are ten customer registers whose contents are maintained in parallel, the description of the benefits of EA should demonstrate cost savings in the form of quality enhancement and decreased labor. After architectural improvement, new customers need to be registered only once rather than ten times. Among other gains, a major benefit involves eliminating the unnecessary time invested in verifying which system's information is correct each time an inconsistency is encountered.

One approach to carrying out a more detailed study about the potential benefits of EA is to calculate the costs of the quality shortcomings. Begin with how important the information is for each process, using, for example, the process and entity group matrix in Figure 1.28. Select an entity group that is strategic or one in which the quality shortcomings will affect senior management.

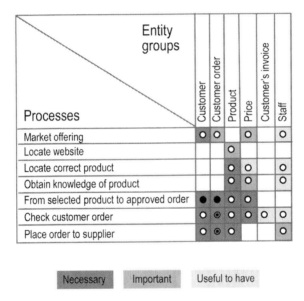

Figure 1.28   Example of weighting information value in the process matrix.

Review the actual data for the entity group and identify how many errors it contains. Calculate how many entity occurrences are inaccurate, incomplete, redundant, etc. Naturally, if there are a million records in a customer database, it will not be possible to examine each entry individually. If this is the case, pick 100 random entries and extrapolate the results.

Calculate the percentage of erroneous occurrences and compare this figure with how often the data is used. It is not at all uncommon for erroneous data to comprise as much as one quarter of the total data in a resource entity register. Prepare a calculation like the simplified one in Figure 1.29. Take into account the extent to which activities in the process use the information and the demand these activities place on resources. A calculation of this kind can result in very large annual sums. Additionally, if the analysis is performed on data from two different systems, the percentage of errors will increase.

Process:	**Perform market activity**
Entity group:	**Customer**
The importance of the information for the process:	**Necessary**
Number of customers:	**1,000,000**
Number of duplicates:	**60,000, 6.0%**
Number of customers with incomplete details:	**47,000, 4.7%**
Number of customers with inaccurate details:	**135,000, 13.5%**
Total quality shortcoming:	**242,000, 24.2%**
Process frequency:	**once a week**
Cost per each process instance:	**€ 100,000**
Cost of quality shortcoming per year:	**€ 1,210,000 (100,000 x 50 times/year x 24.2%)**

Figure 1.29   Example calculation of information quality costs.

Imagine the reverse—that all necessary information is always available and correct. What opportunities would that offer?

Effects on the external environment include altering the business's reputation in terms of credibility and brand name. Additionally, the value of the behavior of the external environment in terms of customer loyalty, supplier accuracy, and so on should be considered. Customer awareness and personalized customer service have become competitive devices, and customers will switch to alternatives if they are dissatisfied with the treatment they receive. An organization that has its information in order internally has a cohesive picture of how it interacts with its customers. It never needs to ask the customer for information the organization already has, and the customer never needs to inform the organization about matters the organization should already be aware of. This adds up to a hassle-free experience for both parties and leads to more satisfied and loyal customers.

Figure 1.30   Doing what we do not do today: thinking outside the box.

Companies with a systems matrix that is 80 percent black, i.e. 80% of its rings are filled, find it difficult to change their processes. In such cases, IT acts as an obstacle rather than a creator of opportunities. Try to estimate the value of performing tasks which are currently lacking in management. It would be possible to change processes more rapidly with the right degree of flexibility in the application portfolio. Greater flexibility makes changing processes simpler and less painful so that the organization can meet external demands quickly and securely.

Assess the benefits of increased opportunities provided by the ideal information supply and a high level of quality. Common benefits include increased insight into customer engagement, greater precision in decision-making, improved follow-up communication, and new opportunities from simpler changes. Use a documented method of analysis to enable comparable benefit studies at later stages.

The system matrix at BestBoatBuilder.com is 97% black (Figure 1.25) and the process matrix is 90% white (Figure 1.23), showing that the system landscape does not meet the process demands. For instance, Customer Order originates in eight systems and Purchase Order in seven. These redundancies mean that each order execution may include fifteen activities instead of one. It is clear that this company cannot grow within its current system landscape. A new one must be formed.

1.4 DESIGNING THE OPTIMUM ARCHITECTURE

An overarching picture is now in place describing the business processes, information needs, and the capacity of the collective systems landscape required to support these processes. Using the insights gained in the previous data analyses, the target architecture can now be designed. The design procedure is carried out in two steps. First, a picture of the ideal architecture is developed. Second, the ideal picture is modified so that it can be realized using available resources and is checked against a number of aspects such as business expectations, ongoing activities, and technical aspects. An optimal architecture is thus achieved, forming the basis for a roadmap. From there, steps to establish the target architecture can be implemented in the correct order.

Using business capabilities

An enterprise architecture can be described clearly and simply with an architecture matrix. This matrix will form the basis for many analyses and decisions later on in the EA process. Therefore, take extra care when conducting this activity to ensure that the matrix is correct and well understood. Create the architecture matrix in a workshop format.

An architecture matrix consists of a set of logical business functions and is guided by a concept that is as simple as it is ingenious: there is no reason to model, specify requirements for, or implement functionality and business rules more than once for each entity group. In other words, there is one function for each entity group that is able to manage all of its data. This single function originates new occurrences and reads, changes, and removes others. We need one, and only one, filled ring (●) per entity group. So, if there is a *Customer Order* entity group, there will automatically be a function called *Manage Customer Order* that has the task of managing information about customer orders. This rule must be followed rigorously; there is only one function that manages customer orders, and that function manages customer orders only. It does not manage *Customers*, for example. This is a strict, information-oriented definition of a *business capability*.

Each entity group forms a business capability. The business capability and entity group relationship is 1:1.

An architecture matrix consists of one column and one row for each entity group, with a filled ring (●) for each combination. Initially, the matrix will have a diagonal line of filled rings from its upper left corner to its lower right. See Figure 1.31.

The basic idea is that data is captured only once at or near the situation where it normally originates. Consequently, there is a business capability that manages how this information is processed and distributed. Do not confuse these business capabilities with organizational functions or systems functions, which may be mapped later on. At this stage, we are forming a neutral architecture based on the business information structure.

Entity groups	1	2	3	5	6	7
Business Capabilities	Customer	Product	Customer Order	Staff	Price	Supplier
1 Manage Customer	●					
2 Manage Product		●				
3 Manage Customer Order			●			
5 Manage Staff				●		
6 Manage Price					●	
7 Manage Supplier						●

Figure 1.31   An empty architecture matrix. The matrix is derived entirely from the entity groups.

For each business capability—that is, for each row in the matrix—mark which information is needed from other entity groups to be able to create a new occurrence. It can be useful to pose the question, "What information is necessary to register a new customer order?" Use an empty ring (O) to mark the entity groups deemed to be providers of necessary information.

According to the example in Figure 1.32, the Customer Order business capability needs information from the Customer, Product, Staff, and Price entity groups.

When completed, the architecture matrix elucidates a number of autonomous business capabilities that have emerged from the normalized information model and are described in terms of information interfaces.

Strive to consider each row individually without examining functional links between them. Maintain the same mental approach while filling in the matrix. It is a good idea to work in pairs, with one facilitator actively working on the matrix while the other assists in maintaining the right focus. Filling in the matrix only on the basis of new occurrences for each entity group keeps the same mental approach throughout the matrix.

Entity Groups / Business Capabilities	1 Customer	2 Product	3 Customer Order	5 Staff	6 Price	7 Supplier
1 Manage Customer	●					
2 Manage Product		●				○
3 Manage Customer order	○	○	●	○	○	
5 Manage Staff				●		
6 Manage Price		○			●	
7 Manage Supplier						●

Figure 1.32   A completed architecture matrix. An empty ring is allocated to the entity groups necessary for the business capability. Note that this matrix may have just a few unfilled rings.

There is a relationship between the architecture matrix and the information model. The rings on a line in the architecture matrix can reoccur as relationships in the information model. As an example, in Figure 1.32 Customer Order has relationships with Customer and Product. However, the architecture matrix need not correspond fully to the information model. It is not necessary for all of the relationships from other entity groups to be represented as empty rings (○) for that business capability. The opposite also applies; not all of the rings on a line need to be represented as relationships since an overarching information model does not need to have all of its relationships sketched in.

When the process and entity group matrix is filled in with empty rings (○), the question is "what information *is needed* to perform the process". A large number of empty rings may be necessary in this case since access to various types of information is required or seen as useful.

In contrast, the architecture matrix asks what information is *necessary* for the business capability, i.e., what information cannot be done without. Using only necessary information results in a matrix that has fewer empty rings, a desirable feature for the upcoming architecture design process.

Think in terms of new occurrences of information entities when filling in the architecture matrix. Assume that new knowledge has just been captured. Examples: a customer has just placed an order, you have just become acquainted with a new customer and been given a business card, you have just decided that a particular bold idea is to become a commercial product.

If there are solution architects aiming for a Service Oriented Architecture (SOA), these business capabilities are great candidates to form SOA services.

Understanding the process and system matrices

To understand the business needs and the current architecture, we need to look more deeply into the matrices produced so far. A closer examination will allow us to estimate the challenge for the coming architecture. Sum up the number of rings (●○) both horizontally and vertically. Study each matrix separately as well as in combination with one another. Pay special attention to the process matrix, as it contains important information about the business structure such as the process dependencies. Processes with empty rings (○) depend on the processes that originate this data. Entity groups without filled rings (●) are depending on processes outside of the city plan's scope or may even be currently missing this data.

A column, i.e. entity group, with many filled rings (●) implies that there are opportunities to reuse functionality. In the process matrix in Figure 1.33, there are two processes creating information about new Products. Managing information about new products could, or maybe even should, be very similar regardless of what process it occurs in. It may be possible to deal with it the same way from an enterprise architecture point of view.

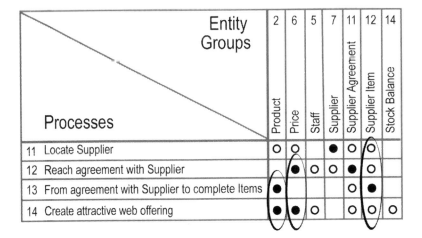

	Entity Groups	2	6	5	7	11	12	14
Processes		Product	Price	Staff	Supplier	Supplier Agreement	Supplier Item	Stock Balance
11	Locate Supplier	O	O		●	O	O	
12	Reach agreement with Supplier		●	O	O	●	O	
13	From agreement with Supplier to complete Items	●				O	●	
14	Create attractive web offering	●	●	O		O	O	O

Figure 1.33 Processes with filled rings in the same column can reuse functionality (entity group 2 & 6). A column with one filled ring and several empty rings indicates that data is reused (entity group 12).

In particular, look at entity groups that are resource entities. If a resource entity is created in just one process and is reused in many others, there exists the potential to reuse information. This makes quality work worth the effort. Conversely, if a resource entity is created in many processes and used in approximately the same number of processes, the risk of disorder is greater. It may be a challenge to identify information sources and to agree on naming, rules, and definitions. It is not as easy to draw general conclusions when it comes to event entities. If an event entity has a filled ring (●) in one process and empty rings (O) in others, it may imply information reuse in different ways. For example, if it is known that an individual occurrence of a Customer Order is created in one process and that particular order is reused in another process, it is obviously more efficient for the correct information to be available to the process with the empty ring (O). However, an empty ring can also represent an aggregation of customer orders. Therefore, it is important to determine the implications of the ring in each individual case.

In the systems matrix, the existence of an entity group column with many filled rings (●) implies that the same information may originate in several systems. A column with many filled rings can also imply redundancy, i.e. different processes storing the same data in different places. Furthermore, several filled rings in a customer entity group column may imply that certain customers are registered in one system and other customers in another. Normally, the existence of redundancies means that there are opportunities for process performance improvements and cost reductions. Large numbers of filled rings throughout the matrix indicate inadequate information ownership, insufficient insight regarding information as a fundamental resource, and the need for rigorous efforts in IT control. A systems matrix with several empty rings (O) suggests that there is extensive integration between systems, while one with few empty rings implies that data is infrequently reused. Few empty rings thus means that business information is not shared and that system keeps useful knowledge isolated.

If the systems matrix has the same pattern as the architecture matrix, the application portfolio is optimal. Ideally, there should be the same number of filled rings (●) in the systems matrix as there are entity groups. If this is the case, we want to express our congratulations and encourage you to start reading another book. However, it is more common for there to be between three and ten times as many filled rings in the systems matrix as there are entity groups (see Figure 1.34). Consequently, the ideal picture is not for the systems matrix to look like the process matrix. That would impede process development.

Compare the system matrix with the process matrix by observing the information requirements of the processes, the extent to which the systems can supply that information, and the level of quality of the information supplied by the systems.

Processes \ Entity Groups	2 Product	6 Price	5 Staff	7 Supplier	11 Supplier Agreement	12 Supplier Item	14 Stock Item
1 Market Offering		o	o	o			
2 Locate Website	o			o		o	
3 Locate correct Product	o	o	o	o		o	
4 Obtain knowledge of Product	o	o	o	o		o	
5 From selected Product to Approved Order	o	o					●
6 Check Customer Order	o	o	o	o	o	o	o
7 Place Order to Supplier	o		o	o	o	o	
8 From Confirmed Order to Delivery to Customer	o	o	o	o	o	o	o
9 From Supplier Invoice to Paid Delivery	o	o	o		o	o	
19 From Customer's Invoice to Payment from Customer	o	o	o	o			
10 Determine Range	●	o		o	o		
11 Locate Supplier	o	o		●	o	o	
12 Reach Agreement with Supplier			●	o	o	●	o
13 From Agreement with Supplier to complete Items	●				o	●	
14 Create Attractive Web Offering	●	●	o		o	o	o
15 Adjust Price and Availability Details	⊙	⊙	o				⊙
16 Manage Staff			●				
17 Provide IT Support			o				
18 Manage Finances	o	o	o		o		o

Systems \ Entity Groups	2 Product	6 Price	5 Staff	7 Supplier	11 Supplier Agreement	12 Supplier Item	14 Stock Balance
1 Web Shop incl. admin	●	●	●	o			
2 SPDS	●	●	●	●		●	
3 aSuperOffice			●				
4 Outlook & Lookout module	●		●				
6 Watif DirectResponse	●	●				●	●
7 Boatstore DirectResponse	●	●				●	●
8 Rudder Web Shop	●	●				●	●
9 Captain Husberg's Internet Store	●	●				●	●
10 BHL Multishipping					●		
11 Kon-Tiki sails	●					●	●
12 Kybernetes	●						
13 Resource Internet Banking							
14 Asping Portal	●	●		●		●	●

Figure 1.34 Comparison between information needs (process/entity groups) on the left and system contents (systems/entity groups) on the right. Processes have extensive information needs and there is a significant amount of information redundancy between systems. Note that not all entity groups are shown in the matrices.

It is a good idea to observe one process at a time and to understand the functions of the systems used in each process. It may be the case that the processes use different systems and are therefore isolated in terms of the information that they each require. If a process, according to the process matrix, has many empty rings it needs to reuse information that is created by other processes. But if it uses systems that have mainly filled rings, this process is probably poorly integrated to other processes.

Significant information isolation between processes is not always noticeable within the business, but is usually apparent from an outside perspective. In such cases, customers, suppliers, and other stakeholders must themselves communicate with the various areas of operations, leading to a disorganized and inefficient business environment.

Present the matrix analysis to the decision makers in an optimistic way. The system matrix can appear to be intimidating and disparaging, two aspects which do not encourage acceptance of the EA message. Therefore, it is well worth it to spend some time refining the results of your analysis. One way to make the matrix analysis more palatable is to present the total difference between the processes' need for information and the information that the system currently contains.

As shown in Figure 1.35, simply add together the different types of symbols in the process matrix and the system matrix and present the proportions of filled and empty rings. The total number of filled rings in the process matrix reflects the number of the required data entry activities, while the total number of filled rings in the system matrix reflects how many redundant activities the system landscape requires. Knowing the number of both of these activities gives the decision makers the ability to visualize the degree of operational inefficiency and the extent of data quality.

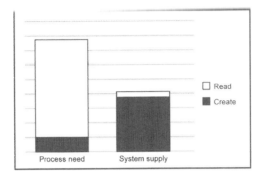

Figure 1.35   Expressing results from matrix analysis showing the processes' need for information and how information is entered in the systems.

Another way to visualize the outcome of the analysis is to combine the entity group business value with the number of system redundancies. The greater the number of filled rings in an entity group in the system matrix, the greater the need for architectural improvement. Mapping these dimensions provides a clear picture of where to start the EA efforts (example in Figure 1.36). This picture is sometimes referred as an "EA heat map."

	Low	Medium	High
High	Supplier Invoice	Customer Customer Invoice	Product Customer Order Stock Balance Price
Medium	Organization	Supplier Staff	Supplier Item Purchase Order
Low	Supplier Agreement		Warehouse Location

Business value (vertical axis) — Need for improvements (horizontal axis)

Figure 1.36   Expressing results from matrix analysis, an "EA heat map."

Sort the architecture matrix so that the empty rings are grouped close to the diagonal path of filled rings (see Figure 1.37). One method of sorting is to start by placing all empty rings beneath (or to the left of) the diagonal. This moves the business capabilities without empty rings to the top of the matrix. Such capabilities manage basic data and may act independently from other business capabilities within the architecture in the future.

Forming ideal blocks in the architecture matrix

Business Capabilities \ Entity Groups	4 Organization	5 Staff	13 Warehouse Location	1 Customer	7 Supplier	11 Supplier Agreement	12 Supplier Item	2 Product	6 Price	3 Customer Order	10 Purchase Order	8 Customer's Invoice	14 Stock Balance	9 Supplier Invoice
4 Manage Organization	●													
5 Manage Staff	○	●												
13 Manage Warehouse Location			●											
1 Manage Customer				●										
7 Manage Supplier					●									
11 Manage Supplier Agreement	○				○	●								
12 Manage Supplier Item					○		●							
2 Manage Product					○		○	●						
6 Manage Price						○	○	○	●					
3 Manage Customer Order		○		○	○		○	○	○	●				
10 Manage Purchase Order						○	○	○	○	○	●			
8 Manage Customer Invoice		○		○				○	○	○		●		
14 Manage Stock Balance			○					○		○	○		●	
9 Manage Supplier Invoice						○		○	○		○			●

Figure 1.37   Sorted architecture matrix; all unfilled rings lie beneath the diagonal.

If an enterprise were to be initiated from the beginning without needing to take into account the operations of older functions, this sorting method would be the correct way to do it. It is best to start with the business capabilities that are the least dependent on information from others (i.e. have the least number of empty rings). Those with the greatest number of empty rings are more dependent on information from other business capabilities and are therefore dealt with last. In this way, the greatest reuse of model structures, information contents, and rules is achieved. Dealing with and implementing one business capability at a time means that each one is only a small addition to the current architecture. The only problem with this information-driven order is that because it does not reflect actual operations particularly well and is not business focused, it needs influences from "reality" before it can be presented as a roadmap to the target enterprise architecture. However, the information-driven order concept can be useful in, for example, determining the order in which modules within a resource planning system should be rolled out or the order in which in-house developed functions should be realized.

From a less theoretical standpoint, we advise you to sort the architecture matrix not only by its patterns but also by its semantic contents. Place entity groups with "strong" relations close to one another and strive to achieve a collective graphical pattern. Allow functional considerations to play a part and group together business capabilities that belong together. Initially, preferences, tastes, and experience may be the main categories for groupings. Try to collect empty rings near the middle of the architecture matrix. The diagonal of filled rings should remain intact throughout the resorting process. Try to think neutrally and dismiss preconceived organizational methods and systems.

Blocks contain the combination of one or more business capabilities. Divided into these blocks, the architecture matrix describes the desired architecture and provides a picture of how it should fit together as a whole. The blocks represent a proposal for how the business capabilities in the architecture matrix should be arranged. A block becomes an initiative and is often equivalent to the scope of a project. A project that takes care of one block will deliver one or more information systems that will cover the functions within that block. Blocks are analogous to quarters or blocks in a city, while the architecture matrix can be thought of as an entire city layout. This comparison holds up rather well; a city is planned block by block, and a city block is built house by house. Therefore, a finished project can deliver a solution for the entire block.

When forming the blocks, start with examining the business's expectations. Return to the needs and operational requirements of the business to ensure that the project's scope is large enough to encompass all of the necessary operations. What is the business model's expected capacity? What are the business's current objectives and how is progress towards meeting these objectives going to be measured? What strategies will have an impact on the bottom line and what processes are considered strategic and especially important in fulfilling the customers' expectations? Below are examples of how businesses encountered by the authors on previous projects have changed:

- An older manufacturer outsourced parts of its product development and all of its production instead of developing and manufacturing internally. It focuses instead on design, branding, and sales.

- A technology company dropped its entire retail operation and its contact with consumers. It enlisted partners to deal with these aspects of the business; these partners changed the products slightly so that they were suitable to consumers in different markets.

- A young business had matured, and it was no longer possible for it to compete on function and production quality. It is now a matter of nurturing relations with the customers who use its products.

- A young trading company left the safety of the inland waterways to venture forth on the world's oceans. Previously, its business operations had involved trade and distribution within one nation, and business development had been synonymous with improvements in the product range. Now, business development involves establishing contacts in new countries with different cultures.

- New legislation will become law in 18 months' time, requiring authorities and companies to radically change their processes and, therefore, their organization and method of reviewing business operations.

- A major public authority previously consisted of autonomous administrative units. In the future, many of its units will be subject to centralized governance, development, and review.

These examples show that the future architecture must be tolerant of currently unknown business initiatives. The challenge of maintaining flexibility in the face of possible changes lies in identifying phenomena that are stable. The business must not be hesitant or unwilling to change tactics when conditions change, and the future architecture must be able to initiate and facilitate dramatic business development.

Divide the architecture matrix into potential blocks. Make these blocks complete squares so that it is easy to see when empty rings end up outside of the blocks, as shown in Figure 1.38. At this stage, the intention is to create independent blocks of information. Assume that a block reflects the scope of an initiative such as a project or a combination of projects in a program. An independent block requires little coordination with other blocks or projects. If you assume that a block represents a system solution, an independent block will require less integration with other blocks.

If an empty ring is located outside and *to the left* of a block, that ring's entity group is necessary for that information block. The block is then depending on information from a block above. If an empty ring is located outside and *above* a block, it is the other way round; another block above is dependent on the information originated by the block.

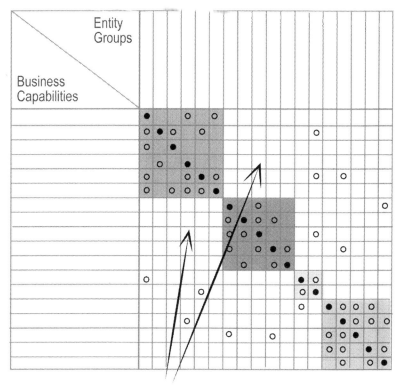

Little or no connection between the blocks

Figure 1.38   Theoretical picture showing areas of few or no rings indicate independent blocks. Rings outside a block indicate need for project coordination or systems integration.

These principles are best understood through an example. In the BesttBoatbuilder.com example in Figure 1.39, three blocks have been formed: an Internal block, a Supplier block, and a Product block. The Supplier block is dependent on the Internal block since the ring that is to the left of the Supplier block and is underneath the Internal block. This is due to the "Manage Supplier Agreement" business capability that needs information about Organization, which belongs to the Internal block. There are rings to the left of the Product block and below the Supplier block. These rings mean that the Product block depends on information from the Supplier block, but not vice versa since there are no rings above the Product block. The Internal and Product blocks are, however, independent from each other.

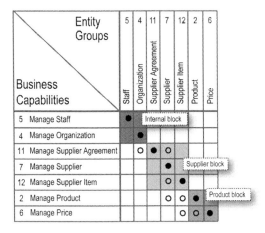

Figure 1.39   Three   blocks   identified   in   the   BestBoatBuilder.com architecture matrix. All rings are successfully placed within a block or below a block.

Now, what does this mean in practice? It means that if these blocks are projects, there would be a need for coordination between the Internal and Supplier projects regarding entity definitions, business rules, and other descriptions about the Organization business capability. The architecture matrix clearly states that it is within the Internal block project that those descriptions should be formed, but such as task has to be coordinated with the Supplier block project. Once these projects deliver systems solutions, the Supplier systems will need to establish an integration contract with the Internal systems regarding the Organization business capability's information. If the projects are not being carried out simultaneously, it is preferable for the Supplier project to be carried out after the Internal project is completed. Otherwise, the Supplier entity would depend on a business capability that is not yet defined. If the Supplier block project is, for whatever reason, completed before the Internal project, the Supplier systems solution may have an insufficient view of the Organization business capability because it has been formed with a sourcing angle of Organization concepts.

Sort the architecture blocks according to how information should be used to carry out these initiatives. One might assume that each block will build up databases and systems within the block. Because the entity groups that are used most frequently will construct the data sets used by other blocks, they need to be established early on in the city plan. The most frequently used blocks are located to the top left in the matrix, while business capabilities requiring access to several other entity groups are located further down in the matrix. When ready, the architecture matrix will show an ideal block organization for the realization of business capabilities that limit the need for coordination and integration.

Forming a realistic architecture

Compare the established blocks in the architecture matrix with the pattern in the process matrix. Take note of which blocks are to be used in the processes by comparing the filled rings in the process and entity group matrix with their corresponding business capabilities in the architecture matrix.

In the right-hand process matrix for BestBoatBuilder.com in Figure 1.40, there is a process called "Reach agreement with supplier." According to the pattern of rings, this process produces information about Supplier agreement and Price. It uses information about Supplier and Supplier item, as indicated by the filled and unfilled rings.

In the left-hand matrix, the Supplier block contains filled rings for Supplier agreement, Supplier, and Supplier Item. Apparently, the Supplier block is capable of managing information about all three and can create, change, and read information. However, prices are managed in the Product block and are not included in the Supplier block.

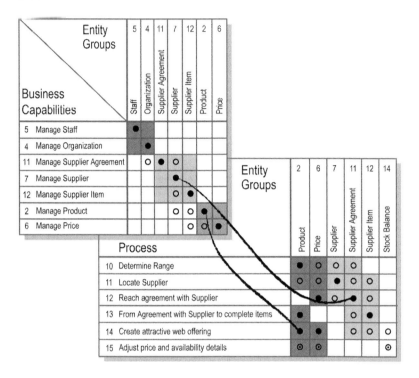

Figure 1.40   The relationship between the architecture blocks and the process matrix. The "Manage Supplier agreement" business capability on the left occurs in the "Reach agreement with supplier" process. The "Manage Product" business capability occurs in the "Create attractive web offering" process.

The consequences from this arrangement may include the following:

- The "Reach agreement with supplier" process will be involved in two projects: first in a project for developing or purchasing systems for the Supplier block and thereafter in a project for the Product block. If projects are to be carried out subsequently, this process will have to work with full systems support until both projects are ready.

- Coworkers who are working in this process may need to work with two information systems. If this would obstruct this process' performance, and maybe even other processes that depend on information in this process, the block design is not ideal.

Assess whether assumed requirements pertaining to the compilation of information and historical data and the maintenance of the data's accuracy are aligned when the same blocks are used in different processes. For example, a sales process manages details on individual customers and has one customer order being processed at a time. The product information that is of interest to the sales process is viewed at the single item level and must always be up to date and accurate. A marketing process, on the other hand, uses information within the Customer Order entity group to examine the total sales volume over several periods, along with the sales totals for different customer categories and products. To a marketing process, trends and patterns are more important than individual details.

Consider the geographical perspective of the blocks by identifying the entity groups captured in different places. Take note of the locations where data are captured. Such places may include warehouses, shops, local offices, vehicles, and central staff units. Take organizational rules into account as well, as certain types of data may have to be determined centrally. Controls may be in place to determine which suppliers are to be used, the specific products that are to be ordered, and what customer groups are applied.

The considerations above may lead to a reorganized architecture matrix. Blocks might be split into smaller ones, and business capabilities might be moved from one block to another or be separated to form new blocks.

Each empty ring located outside a block indicates a need for integration. The existence of several blocks means that the squares will be smaller and there will be more rings outside the blocks. Fewer, and thus larger, blocks will include most of the rings inside the squares, implying a lower need for integration. As this is a strictly information centric proposal for an ideal application portfolio, a decision has to be made about how many blocks are needed and the degree to which those blocks are integrated. Dividing the architecture matrix into blocks controls the scope of both the projects' and the systems' solutions.

Integration specialist Dave McComb has come up with an interesting correlation between the cost of developing systems and the cost of their integration:

- The fewer systems an organization has, the more expensive it is to develop or acquire them.
- Conversely, the more systems you have, the lower the total cost of developing them.

As shown in Figure 1.41, the total cost of developing systems would be very high if all of the functions and information were gathered in just two systems.

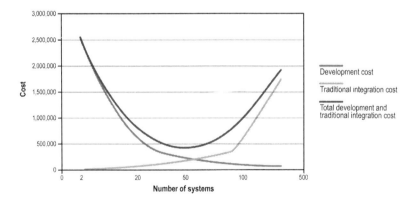

Figure 1.41   The correlation between number of systems and cost of new acquisition or integration. © Dave McComb. Used with permission.

Creating these two systems would be an extremely complex task. It would form two giant projects, or rather programs, each with very wide scope. It would entail numerous conflicting requirements from stakeholders, and it would require a complicated development process with laborious implementation.

Electing instead to obtain several smaller systems that have the same total functionality makes it easier to monitor the development of each system, which lowers the level of risk of each project. Consequently, the total cost of obtaining new systems falls as the number of systems increases.

Unfortunately, the cost of integration increases as the number of systems becomes larger. Similarly, the need for coordination between the business analysis and process improvements preceding the systems also increases since there will be a large amount of concurrent business development work going on.

According to McComb, there is a "comfortable medium" between the number of systems and the degree of integration, meaning that there are a sufficient number of systems as well as low integration costs. According to Figure 1.41, among the companies surveyed this comfortable medium involved 40-100 systems.

It is hard to provide a general recommendation as to how many systems a larger company should have. However, one should strive to keep integration costs low. One way of reducing these costs is to create common and coherent set of data definitions that, with the help of information modeling, captures and assesses how well the new systems function.

If the information that is common for the entire organization was readily available to all systems, integration would be considerably easier. Keeping a check on critical entity groups with extensive integration needs is a main architectural task.

The existence of numerous blocks in the architecture matrix means that the systems will be smaller. Smaller systems provide opportunities for more flexible processes since they are not "entwined" in large systems. Smaller systems are easier and cheaper to change. However, as mentioned previously, the existence of too many systems leads to higher integration costs and a greater need for coordination. Therefore, use the architecture matrix to visualize and establish block sizes and integration complexity at levels that seem easily manageable.

Check the relevance of entity groups that are considered to be strategically important in the architecture matrix against any completed preliminary work. This work includes the business model canvas, unique process requirements, key success factors for target achievement, prioritized customer values, and strategically important processes.

Produce a summary description of the blocks. Try to determine whether a whole block (or one of its business capabilities) may be outsourced, created using a standard package, or developed in-house. For sensitive data that should not leave the organization, the business capability for acquiring these data (●) may not be outsourced although it may be possible to implement it using a standard software package.

The result from the considerations above may look like the architecture in Figure 1.42. It is a set of business capabilities, each of which is derived from an enterprise business information model and grouped into blocks.

Important information dependencies between the capabilities are clearly marked and therefore also possible to handle. This is a target enterprise architecture that is neutral to existing systems and to today's organizational structures.

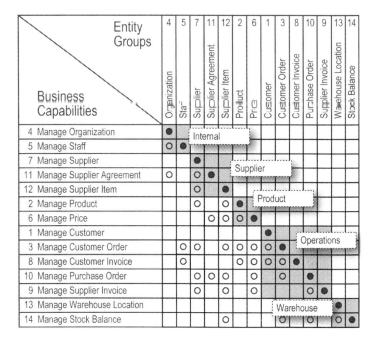

Figure 1.42   The result: a target enterprise architecture with business capabilities grouped into blocks.

1.5 PLANNING THE ENTERPRISE ARCHITECTURE DELIVERABLES

The optimum architecture for the organization has now been described. It is visionary and is based on the processes' needs along with a neutral business information structure. Together with the business's requirements, consideration of actual conditions, and integration assessments, the optimum architecture has become a realistic target scenario that can now be gradually implemented. This final part of the "Ready" step deals with establishing the architecture's development path. The city plan includes the process for how the architecture is to be realized—the roadmap for development and phasing-out of business and systems. It also addresses how the enterprise architect's deliveries are to be made and the responsibilities that he or she is to take on in the short term.

Short-term EA planning

Start with understanding the gaps between the new target architecture and its systems and ongoing projects. Make a list of the projects that are already initiated and compare the planned blocks with these projects and with key existing systems. Identify overlaps and gaps between the blocks and projects in preparation for discussing the project's scope and integration plans. Make an assessment of how current projects and existing systems fit into the new optimum block picture. It may be the case that several blocks and projects will have to be left out of the final architecture.

Compare the goals of the projects that are already underway with current strategies and overarching objectives of the enterprise. Decide which of the blocks and current projects are the most crucial to have finished in the short term. Introducing new systems at this point will weaken the overall picture, so determine how these systems relate to the block picture and how they will affect it. Make a short term plan from this gap analysis that addresses how these projects and new systems can adapt to the new target architecture.

Long-term EA planning

Establish a long-term plan for a development sequence that is based on the blocks in the architecture matrix. Each block will replace a number of older systems. The order in which old systems are phased out should be connected to the long-term development plan so that it is easy to see which systems are to be replaced by which blocks (see Figure 1.43).

The architecture matrix is formed with information dependency in mind and is then grouped by business capabilities and process needs.

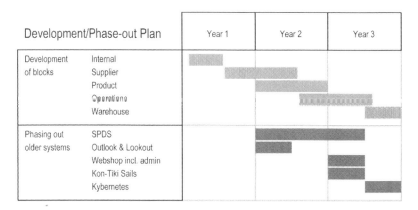

Development/Phase-out Plan		Year 1	Year 2	Year 3
Development of blocks	Internal			
	Supplier			
	Product			
	Operations			
	Warehouse			
Phasing out older systems	SPDS			
	Outlook & Lookout			
	Webshop incl. admin			
	Kon-Tiki Sails			
	Kybernetes			

Figure 1.43   The blocks from Figure 1.42 laid out as a long-term plan.

There are several other noteworthy parameters to take into account when making a long-term plan that establishes a timeline for the blocks:

- The order in which the blocks are realized should be based not only on informational dependencies and technical plans, but also on prioritized processes. Knowing which processes to begin with means that it is possible to indicate, based on the process and entity group matrix, what information you need in order to start your plan. Remember to progress via the architecture and try to avoid examining the needs of individual processes by themselves.

- Determine if you have access to the expertise and resources that are necessary for beginning with the highest-priority process. Do analyses about current trends and business developments have anything to say about where you should start so that you can keep up with external changes?

- Does the IT strategy say anything about the technology that should be prioritized or phased out? If so, do these changes affect the order in which the blocks should be constructed?

Indicate the intended order for the blocks' development in the plan. For each block, specify the processes, business capabilities, entity groups and existing systems that are affected. The responsibility for each block, when considered as a planned project, encompasses the requirements for functions in the new system and responsibility for modeling business information entities. Also, be sure to state which entity groups will be reused from existing systems, planned systems, or parallel projects.

The development plans include a rough description of what is required of the business for it to be successful in its development and phase-out activities. The process of securing support and expertise is explained in greater detail in the next chapter, which includes a plan regarding how the envisaged development and phase-out plans are to be staffed and scheduled.

Establishing a roadmap

An architecture development plan must be ended with a phase-out plan. If the driving force behind the architecture process is information quality, phase-out needs are particularly important for decreasing redundant information acquisition. The method for constructing a phase-out plan that maintains the desired data storage efficiency is simple and comes from the theory that the architecture matrix should only include one filled ring per entity group.

Go through the entity groups in the systems matrix and formulate a definition of the information's "true source" for each group. A true source is where the information, or rather the knowledge, arises for the first time. For information that originates within the organization, such as the price of an item, the true source is an activity within a process that is often performed by a single person. This activity can, for example, be a pricing decision. For information that arises outside of the organization, such as a supplier's bank account number, there is no way to control how the information originates. For situations involving other businesses, it is important to have confidence in their information. However, confidence alone may not be enough; in many cases it is necessary to have a procedure in order to check the information for errors once it reaches your organization.

It is important to realize that the definition of the true information source is based on operational business events and not on a particular system. This key distinction brings us to the next task: to find or create a system in which new information will be captured and stored. In the systems matrix, mark which systems are to act as original sources for each entity group. It is not necessary for each entity group to have a systems source marked in the systems matrix. Certain entity groups can have an information source in one of the systems that will be developed by a planned block.

During a transitional period, more than one system may act as a source. For example, there might be one system for private customers and another for corporate customers. If a multi-source structure is to remain the same in the future, it is helpful to form two entity groups so that differences between the information sources can be clarified.

It is theoretically possible to phase out all systems that do not contribute anything to the business's overall information supply. In order to eliminate only the non-contributing systems, we must begin assessing their information contributions. If a process is supported by a system that provides inaccurate information, there is room for lowering costs and improving performance. Reducing the prevalence of inaccurate information in a system leads to lower costs and improves the bottom line for companies that invest in improved systems support. Improved systems support can come from the integration of new and old of systems in accordance with the ideal architecture.

Compiling a city plan

Document your observations and questions as you continue developing the architecture. Compile the material in a report and in one or more presentations. Prepare proposals for decisions to be made by the senior management team and express an expectation of management's commitment.

Having a city plan is fundamental even when forming service-oriented solutions. Use the business capabilities in the enterprise architecture to form the services.

Determine if the city plan is a strategic document in its own right or if it should be part of an existing document. Merging the city plan into existing strategy documents often means it will be divided into both business and IT plans.

Present the report to the sponsor and to the senior management team. Adapt the presentations to the target audiences; not everyone is equally interested in, for example, information models and matrices.

Allow the senior management team to reach a decision on the project's continuation. Present and disseminate the contents of the city plan to the rest of the organization in a suitable manner.

1.6 SUMMARY OF THE READY STEP

Below are the major steps in the "Ready" method described in this chapter. The numbers in the following list refer to the method result overview in Figure 1.44.

Begin by determining which of the business's expectations will be met by the target enterprise architecture. Use business innovation models, such as the Business Model Canvas, to decide which type of enterprise you will form.

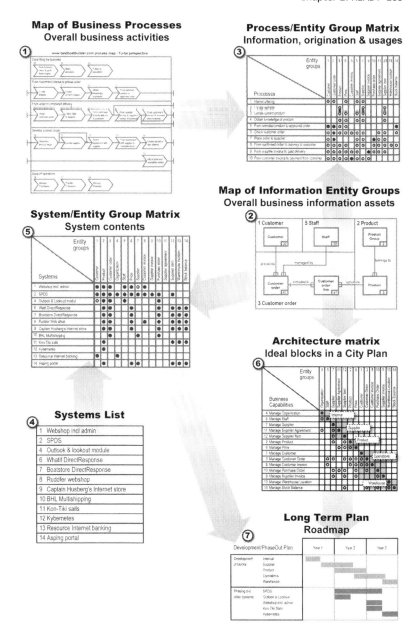

Figure 1.44   Results in the Ready overview

Produce a high-level process map ① containing end-to-end process chains. This map reflects a "to-be" perspective that will meet business expectations that are neutral in regards to organizational structures.

Produce a high-level business information model (entity group model) ② in two steps:

1. Produce an overall business information model that uses the traditional entity-relationship modeling technique while reflecting a business perspective rather than a database design. Make sure that this model shows a "to-be" perspective and does not include only the existing systems.
2. Group the entities in this model into entity groups.

Combine the high-level process map and high-level business information model into a process matrix ③ using only two symbols that show that the process creates (originates) business information (●) or that the process reads (uses) business information (○).

Gather a list of systems ④ that are commonly used. Make a note of the technology used and if there is a possible "best-before" date for any of the systems.

Combine the systems list and the high-level information business model into a system matrix ⑤ by using the same symbols as before. At this stage, you have captured an overview of your current enterprise architecture.

Form the target architecture ⑥ using the following steps:

1. Let each entity group form a business capability. Call these business capabilities "Manage" + entity group name. For example, "Manage Stock" and "Manage Customer Order."
2. Describe each business capability in an architecture matrix that shows which other entity groups are necessary for each business capability (using the simple symbol ○).
3. Group the capabilities into blocks. A block may correspond to a project, a system or a group of systems, or a service.

Compile a city plan that includes the results produced above with the target architecture roadmap ⑦. The roadmap contains a plan for upcoming business development initiatives and a phase-out plan for older systems.

Now we are "Ready." Let's get "Set"!

Chapter 2
SET

Summary of activities in *Set*:

Identifying stakeholders and target groups:
- Conducting a SWOT analysis by analyzing strengths, weaknesses, opportunities, and threats
- Formulating targets for EA
- Securing the support of management and other necessary people in the organization.

Forming an EA-oriented development environment:
- Establishing EA in business development
- Establishing EA in IT visions and IT strategy
- Establishing EA in IT planning
- Establishing EA in project execution.

Forming the EA ownership:
- Finding an owner and a manager
- Assigning responsibilities
- Forming a decision process.

Organizing the enterprise architects:
- Describing their roles, mandates, and responsibilities
- Describing competence needs and recruiting
- Establishing rules for the prioritization of development projects
- Identifying EA triggers and warnings.

Identifying requirements for EA tools:
- Forming meta-models for model management and EA results
- Identifying rules for models.

Communicating and planning:
- Communicating Key Success Factors.

GETTING SET

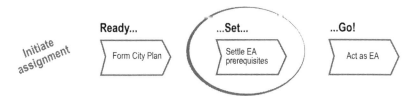

Figure 2.1   Step "Settle EA prerequisites" in the method chain.

Enterprise architecture is primarily about change. An enterprise's architecture is affected whenever the business or its environments change; inserting an EA mindset into a business environment is a significant change in itself. The following process, called *Settle EA Prerequisites*, deals with paving the way for the introduction of enterprise architecture, therefore allowing the introduction to be successful. This process involves organizing an architecture team, along with its working methods. The following activities do not need to take place in the order mentioned here and should instead happen in an order that is based on the company's needs. See Figure 2.2.

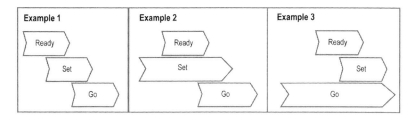

Figure 2.2   Three examples of EA implementation

- Example 1: Begin by constructing the city plan in order to get the necessary information and to visualize your business's needs. Continue the process by setting up your prerequisites after which you can finally start the actual EA work.

- Example 2: Begin by recruiting an Enterprise Architect. The next task is to form the city plan, after which starts the actual EA work.

- Example 3: Start the EA work in practice by using in-house competence with support from consultants. After a while, it will become necessity to form a city plan. Finally, EA resources and other prerequisites will be formally established.

Ideally, one should perform the EA implementation as in Example 1 that is, by following the approach described in this book. However, EA implementation is, in practice, often carried out in the sequences described in Examples 2 and 3.

Before you begin the implementation process, review the critical success factors developed in the initiation of the city plan. Select the factors that are the most necessary for success and ensure that the preparations will allow them to be enacted.

2.1 IDENTIFYING STAKEHOLDERS AND TARGET GROUPS

Find the groups and individuals within the organization who are recipients (those who are directly affected by the result) of the EA work, along with those who will be most affected by a well-organized architecture. Find high-ranking representatives within the organization, such as those in upper management or on the board of directors. Product and business developers may also be useful contacts. All of the groups mentioned above are referred to as *stakeholders* in the following text.

Project managers, the CIO, and IT architects are often the primary target groups for EA work. External customers and organizations that are partners can also be stakeholders. Try to ascertain how their everyday lives can be improved by EA, identify explicitly the additional value that EA will contribute (higher data quality, reuse, etc.), and be able to demonstrate how this added value can be realized.

It is also a good idea to find a sponsor for EA in a senior management position. This person could be:

- Someone with experience working in earlier architecture processes in other organizations
- A person with extensive experience in the business and with good insight into its problems.

The sponsor does not need to work directly to build the architecture, but they need to understand its effects. They may be the person responsible for directing the EA work or they might find it more time-efficient to delegate the details to project leaders. The principal reason for having a sponsor is to guarantee stability in connection with future reorganization and transfers of power. Identify a suitable individual in management who could act as a promoter of the EA work.

Greater support is often needed in connection with changes than is provided by sponsors. For this reason, it is helpful to appoint managers who deal specifically with the effects of changes brought on by implementing a new architecture. These people should be available to all individuals affected by long-term enterprise architecture efforts.

Change management takes place at different levels. Sponsors, who often work at a higher organizational level, communicate the benefits and business advantages of working architecturally to the people at their level in the business. At the general employee level, coaches and change managers work to motivate, encourage, and explain what the changes mean on a personal level. They need to answer questions such as:

- How will I be affected by these changes?
- Can I do this?

- What's in it for me?

The process map can be a good starting point. Focus on the processes that will change significantly and identify the stakeholders that will be the most affected.

Read as much as you can about the senior management team, their business plans, and the key issues facing the business. Produce presentation material that clearly describes the benefits of enterprise architecture for management. Schedule a meeting to present your material and start a dialogue.

Conducting a SWOT analysis: analyzing strengths, weaknesses, opportunities, and threats

Analyze possible obstacles to beginning the implementation process. Such obstacles can be discovered through various methods, one of which entails conducting a SWOT analysis, which will be discussed later on in this chapter. When formulating your EA implementation plan, ensure sufficient scope for dealing with possible obstacles. Consider what your organization is ready for and has time for. Emphasize the beneficial aspects of the implementation plan, and make sure that the benefits are clearly linked to business entities and business strategies. Carry out this work with a group of business representatives who are, preferably, members of future target groups.

Formulating targets for EA

A key success factor for EA work is to set targets that are measurable and communicate these targets frequently and to a broad audience. If communication is not frequent enough or all-encompassing, there is a risk that the EA work will be de-prioritized since the effects of the process are long term and may not be visible to most employees during the short term. Determine the following before setting targets:

- What is your EA vision and strategy?
- How will the development process appear at a future point when an enterprise-wide perspective is achieved rather than a project-focused view?
- What competencies does the EA work require?
- What reporting channels will you be using?

It is preferable to start with a small number of targets that can be measured and whose effects are soon apparent. Communicate your progress and results to the sponsor and other stakeholders on an ongoing basis.

Formulate targets for the EA work, both for the long-term and for a one-year horizon or even shorter period. These targets should be measurable and linked to the overarching business plan for the enterprise.

Separate the internal EA targets from the external ones. Example target separation:

- The external targets will measure how the architecture can contribute to the business by, for example, reducing the degree of redundant information acquisition and reuse, reducing the number of "extinguished" rings in the system matrix, and improving perceived flexibility during changes.
- Internal targets deal with the performance of the architecture itself and include completing modeling sessions, project participation, performing service for different projects, and so forth.

Furthermore, there are EA maturity targets that indicate if EA is accepted as such and adopted in business and IT development.

Securing support from management

To carry out a successful implementation of enterprise architecture, support for the necessary changes is needed from both senior management and the key stakeholders in the organization. The city plan report is often a substantial document that takes time to digest. Consequently, it is recommended that the enterprise architect begins his or her dialogue with the management and stakeholders by showing them the most important insights from the city plan and, based on these points, talking about examples of the benefits of the proposed measures. Also, outline current challenges and areas of focus and describe how the enterprise architecture can help to resolve these problems.

2.2 FORMING AN EA-ORIENTED DEVELOPMENT ENVIRONMENT

EA activities in business development

Every enterprise has, to some extent, a business vision and strategy as the base for their future plans. Every planned business advantage, change, and reduction needs to be aligned with both EA and IT planning. The three plans in Figure 2.3 are the Business plan, the EA plan, and the IT plan, and all are derived from visions and strategies; there must be a clear connection between each of them.

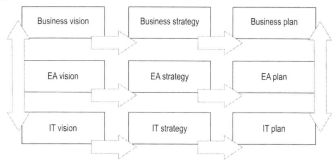

Figure 2.3   A framework for connecting business planning to EA and IT planning. Examples of various governing documents, from business vision to an IT plan. Adapted from Rune Brandinger. Used with permission.

Ideally, there is one vision document and one strategy document covering all three perspectives. Typically, the EA vision and strategy statements are included in the Business plan, the IT plan, or even in both.

Business visions, strategies and plans have different timescales. Business visions are endless, strategies look ahead to the next four or five years, and business plans describe what to do in the next month or year. The EA plan is an operative plan covering what the enterprise architects should do during the subsequent six to twelve months. The activities in the EA plan, along with the business and IT plans, need to be aligned with the city plan and its roadmap. Aligning all of these plans increases the enterprise architect's possibilities to be well prepared for participating in the early stages of development initiatives. Try to understand the underlying business objectives and benefits for each initiative, not just the objectives' obvious results. The initiatives will probably form projects, which tend to focus mainly on results and may lose track of the objectives that are the motivating force behind producing results.

EA work in business development might include the following:

- Mapping business innovations to the processes, the information objects, and the matrices in the city plan. The Business Model Canvas (explained in the previous chapter) is a useful tool for communicating with innovators, as changes in the business model will most certainly affect the business's processes, information definitions, and systems.
- Suggesting areas of improvements from findings in the city plan.
- Detecting conflicting or unaligned initiatives.
- Visualizing operational changes in process or activity diagrams.

- Providing and maintaining an all-encompassing enterprise perspective while working with narrow and detailed business designs.

EA activities when forming an IT vision and IT strategy

The technical visions and strategies for the business usually include goals, principles and restrictions for deliveries of applications, and services from the IT department. The IT strategy should also include a target application landscape (which includes a vision of what applications you want to have), as well as a roadmap detailing how to reach that landscape. The target landscape should be based on, or at least derived from, the city plan, which gives suggestions for the ideal application portfolio. The development/phase-out plan provides an ideal roadmap that includes both wanted and unwanted systems.

EA activities to perform when forming EA and IT plans

An IT plan usually has the form of a project portfolio and is applied on a medium-length timeframe. It is typically produced by a CIO when budgeting next year's work and is continuously updated. The IT plan should be a collection of project definitions, including the business's objectives and scope, the business objectives' order of execution, the extent of the business's coordination needs, and the architecture prerequisites for each project. Make sure that the projects' portfolio plans include mapping entity groups to intended projects. Doing this will help to identify commonalities between information modeling and project specification and will allow for the completion of necessary activities prior to the development of these projects. Plan for a reduction in overlaps between multiple sources.

Plan out the activities that will be initiated by the enterprise architect—for example, the elaboration of entity groups that will be used in several projects (e.g. Product, Staff, Customer Order). Compile an overall EA-plan based on project and EA needs.

The following constructions will help you develop an EA plan:

- The business plan
- The development and phase-out plan (one short-term and one long-term)
- A list of planned and current projects
- The business's own initiatives
- The city plan.

EA activities when executing development projects

For the enterprise architecture approach to be successful, you must maintain a holistic perspective, keeping the entire enterprise in mind when making any decisions or changes. The project management approach usually focuses on activities and results for one project. Therefore, the project management model needs to include EA checkpoints that provide those working on projects with an enterprise-wide view. It is essential that the architect is included in the project management work from an early stage and that he or she has the opportunity to check that the initiative the project group is working on is in line with the envisaged direction of the business. Ensure that the project's results will both enhance the overall picture and contribute to the EA objectives. Similarly, the project should not address matters already being dealt with by another project; each one should be able to reuse existing results and make their own results available to other project groups.

The project management model requires that the people working on each project specify their expected results and the benefits they plan to produce. Furthermore, project managers should specify the target results of their projects by, for example, listing current and future process descriptions, problems they come across, information models their project is using, etc. The project management model indicates the decision points or milestones that are applied to the architecture such as checks and quality assurance.

An EA-adopted development model includes the following activities:

- Construct the information models from a business perspective. Involve the interested parties from other processes that are both upstream and downstream in the modeling process by consulting the process matrix. This matrix shows which processes are information suppliers or consumers for common information entities.

- Involve managers and representatives from areas depending on the analysis of the information models. Consult the architecture matrix to understand the dependencies between modeled entities within the scope of the project.

- Study common information models and reuse standardized structures. Plan detailed modeling activities for the models' missing parts.

- Form a detailed target information structure that includes entities, attributes, definitions, and constraints in a lifecycle perspective. Use language and diagrams that are easily digestible for the business's employees.

- Verify the business models by using examples, and validate the models by translating the graphical models into text.

- When applicable, address the need for improved common structures rather than attempting to work around old inefficiencies.

- When purchasing a new application, perform reverse engineering on previously purchased applications (COTS = Commercial Off-The-Shelf) and map their structures against the common architectural information structure. Identify and document gaps and differences in the structures and their regulations.

- When reusing applications, map the application model against the reused structure. Identify any gaps in the old and new application structures.

- When building or designing a solution for the business information structure, implement data storage according to the design of the common architecture structure. At this stage it is acceptable to begin using an IT-oriented graphical language (such as UML).

- Audit and document the usage and integration of the common architecture.

- Integrate master data to appointed data sources using a standard integration format.

- Make the final versions of your models and definitions available throughout the business. Publish this information so that it can easily be found.

If you plan ahead and work pro-actively during the projects' early stages, you will not have to spend valuable time making significant revisions close to the projects' deadlines.

Often, project management models lack a description of how business operations and IT should be developed. Many organizations end up using the same project management model for remodeling office space, developing new products, or acquiring new business systems. In such cases, the business needs an EA-adapted development model that describes how architecture-driven development is carried out and how it connects to the project management model.

Hints

- Determine which project management model is currently being used. Plan the EA activities to arrive at an optimal development process with an overall view for the business's development.

- Establish criteria that determine which projects are to be prioritized.

- Establish rules regarding the level of commitment of key personnel.

- Set requirements and timelines for the projects.

2.3 FORMING THE EA OWNERSHIP

EA introductions are often complex and vague. Its value is hard to communicate and too often the problems EA attempts to solve become just more issues for IT to deal with. Therefore, a clear, non-disputable, and personal principle is very useful.

The basic principle: derive information definition and ownership from its origination point.

An EA entity definition, as well as its implementation and ownership, derives from where its entity occurrences originate. When applied, this principle has proven to be both useful and powerful.

- **Definition.** The definition of a business information entity comes from the business situation in which the information originally arises. For instance, define the

Customer entity in the context in which someone becomes a customer. It is in this context of becoming a customer that the definition becomes alive. You will find the most useful business knowledge within real-world business situations.

- **Implementation considerations.** "Should we initiate the project for a new customer database before the sales system is complete?" It is difficult to create a Sales Order without first having a Customer or a Product. Therefore, projects dealing with Customers and Products need to be finished first.

- **Ownership.** Find the owner of an entity in the same context in which the entity is defined.

By using filled and empty rings, the matrices in the previous chapter show the processes and systems that capture and reuse each business entity:

- The symbol for Create (●) includes establishing, reading, changing, and removing individual entity occurrences. This is the business context in which you should establish the entity's precise definition, describe procedures and business rules, and list its IT requirements.

- The symbol for Read (○) reads one entity occurrence at a time or a compilation of several occurrences. This is the point at which you should find stakeholders who rely on the information supply. Involve them in the work by showing them benefits that result from the EA work.

In the architecture matrix, you can find entity dependencies that show the order in which the entities need to be created. Using dependencies to establish the entity creation order is useful when forming a governance model for EA. It becomes easier to find suitable owners, managers, and stakeholders.

Entity owner and entity manager

To be able to continue the EA initiative and carry out the city plan, entity owners need to be appointed. As the name would suggest, an entity owner owns entity groups and all of their connected entities, attributes, relationships, and constraints. An entity owner can own one or more entity groups depending on their level of expertise and responsibility. It is not necessary for them to be an IT solution owner. An entity owner should have wide business experience of the information within the entity that they are responsible for.

An entity owner's responsibilities cover a wide range of activities including:

- Determining the scope (i.e., range, domain) for each group
- Setting goals for business information quality
- Appointing entity managers
- Raising funding for the work performed by the entity managers and architects
- Approving information structures and solutions.

The position of entity owner is, however, not only a formal role. He or she is also the person who encourages, supports, and prepares the working space for the entity managers. The entity owner must be aware of the challenges that the entity managers will be faced with in order to be helpful.

The role and skills of an entity manager are as diverse and important as those of the entity owner. An entity manager is responsible for ensuring that the entity models are correct and that the information within the models is described correctly. An entity manager prepares changes for the owners, who then approve the changes prior to implementation. An entity manager's skills should include the following:

- Profound business knowledge, especially about the context in which the entity information arises
- An information lifecycle perspective
- An analytical mindset
- An understanding of the value of well-organized architecture
- Basic information modeling skills although he or she need not be an expert in this area.

The entity manager has the following responsibilities:

- Correctly describing the entity groups
- Ensuring that the definitions of the entities are correct and up to date
- Updating models when changes take place in business operations
- Ensuring that data quality procedures are accurate and implemented in a timely fashion.

The entity manager fully understands everything in the entity group detail model and has knowledge about the contents in adjacent entity groups. An enterprise architect prepares the entity managers work by producing valid entity definitions including constraints, category values, attributes, and identifiers, as shown in Figure 2.4.

A complete entity description includes detailed processes or procedures for how to capture, update, and clean entity occurrences. A data quality governance model also requires instructions for confirming data completeness and accuracy. The entity manager needs to monitor ownership on the data level by, for example, making sure that every record in a customer database is accurate and that data quality procedures are followed. The above mentioned activities are the most common tasks within a pool of management responsibilities for master data.

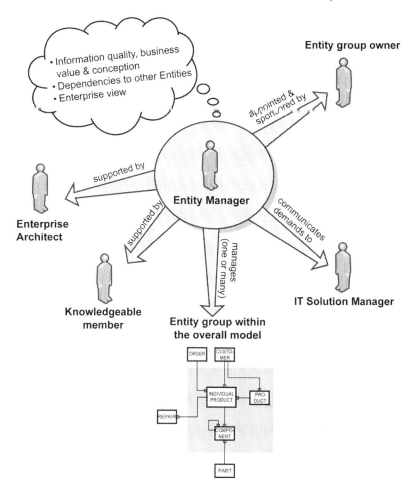

Figure 2.4   The entity manager.

In addition to all of these tasks and responsibilities, an entity manager needs to be aware of the system matrix for his or her entities and stay up to date in regards to knowing which entities occur within which systems, as well as what should or should not occur, or should occur differently. It is helpful to know about the current and planned projects that will be working with the entity group.

Begin the process of forming the architecture's ownership by identifying the entity managers. Look for them while going through the modeling process with business representatives. Those who have solid business knowledge, understand the diagrams, and want to improve information quality are ideal candidates. If there is not an obvious owner, let the entity manager's boss be the owner.

Hints

- Let your EA governance also be your data quality governance.

- Avoid political influences when assigning architecture's ownerships.

Regardless of whether you own a model, an entity group, or a SOA service, it is important to bear in mind that what you own functions not only within a particular system, but is also part of a larger whole. It may therefore be useful not to appoint persons who also are systems owners.

Although it is common to assign process owners to information ownership positions, it is not recommended to do so since processes are changed more frequently than the business information structure. It is better practice to give ownership roles to individuals with broad expertise within the entity groups.

Who decides, who influences?

A governance model only works well if it is unused. Every time a conflict about an issue in the organization escalates, it is a failure for the governance model since if the model works, this conflict would not arise. It is better to do things correctly from the beginning. One way to make sure you start off on the right foot is to have a way to ensure that when one person or group makes a change in one place in the architecture, others who are affected are alerted to the change and have the capability to deal with its effects.

As stated in the previous chapter, the architecture matrix shows the entities that must already exist before adding in a new entity occurrence. However, the architecture matrix does not show only this functional information demand. It also highlights the need for entity groups to have common definitions. As mentioned earlier, the architecture matrix forms the base for application planning along with the dependency rules for ownership and governance.

The architecture matrix in Figure 2.5 shows that when a new Customer Invoice is created (as indicated with a black dot), information about Product, Customer, Price, and Customer Order must be available before the Customer invoice is created. This is because a new invoice needs information about Product, Customer, Price, and Customer Order to be able to create the invoice (as indicated by the white dots). The new invoice's relation to the existing functions implies that the entity manager for the Customer invoice entity needs approval from the Product, Customer, Price, and Customer Order entity managers when determining how their entities are included in the Customer invoice entity.

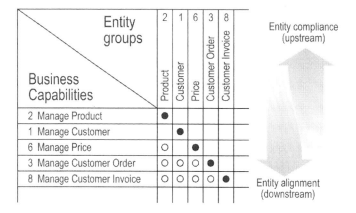

Figure 2.5   The architecture matrix as a base for governance. The empty
rings suggest, or even determine, who depends on whom.

Transform the architecture matrix into a dependency scheme to make it easier to understand, as shown in Figure 2.6.

Dependent \ Depending on		Who relies on me? Where should I align and anchor my definition? (downstream)				
		Product	Customer	Price	Customer Order	Customer Invoice
To whom do I comply? (upstream)	Product					
	Customer					
	Price	✓				
	Customer Order	✓	✓	✓		
	Customer Invoice	✓	✓	✓	✓	

Figure 2.6   The architecture matrix transformed into a dependency scheme.

Form a decision process

An EA governance model needs a forum for making decisions. Without a way to centralize the decision-making process, there is a risk that EA matters will be decided within the projects' steering committees. The end result of making decisions in this manner is a sub-optimal situation that, in the long term, will lead to inflexible systems support and poor information quality. While most organizations have clear decision-making channels for projects, EA work requires a decision-making forum with an overall view and that has the ability to make decisions about issues outside of the scope of individual projects.

The following are examples of decision-making bodies for architectural matters:

- Company management, management's appointed representatives, or the board of directors.
- A prioritization committee consisting of the owners of key business processes or other appointees with a broad knowledge of the business.

The decision-making body needs to hold frequent meetings so that business improvement initiatives are not delayed by coordination requirements. The enterprise architect should express in clear terms what is needed so that they know what warning signs to look for.

Hints

- Describe the entity and entity manager roles with attributes and knowledge requirements, and formulate profiles of the individuals needed.
- Make an inventory of the expertise that currently exists within the organization and compare this with the needs that exist.
- Highlight any gaps in expertise or experience. Where necessary, formulate internal or external job advertisements to eliminate these gaps.
- Hire the necessary people.
- Make sure that the entity dependency scheme is considered during the decision-making process.

There may be situations about which the enterprise architect needs to consult the decision-making body, and the decision makers need to know what to report to the architect in such situations. Tell the project managers (or other important people) that the decision-making forum is where such issues are to be discussed, prepared, and resolved.

Describe the process by which such decisions, including referrals, are prepared before EA matters are addressed by a decision-making body. An example would be the decisions about which project should create data if there are many projects within the same area. Use templates and checklists for agendas and decision proposals to facilitate the decision-making process.

2.4 ORGANIZING THE ENTERPRISE ARCHITECTS

Formulate how the EA work should proceed so that you can achieve your measurable architectural targets. You can determine this schedule yourself or use established methods as your basis, adapting them to the needs of the organization. If there is a project management model in your organization, check how closely it agrees with the EA work and if the EA targets can actually be achieved with the model's working method. A good way to describe how the work should be carried out is to describe it in a process augmented with checklists. Check up on the work as it is being completed to ensure that the process you have chosen is being followed.

Describing roles, mandates, and responsibilities

Distribute tasks and activities for EA work by assigning roles such as assignor, business architect, requirements analyst, and IT architect. Describe the roles fully and link their responsibilities to both the activities in the processes that have been described here and to the architectural targets. Define the responsibilities of the roles and which authorizations they need (for example, the authority to stop a project that does not reuse information) to be able to meet their targets. Although an individual can have several competencies, it is uncommon for a single individual to have all of the necessary competencies.

An organization needs employees who work with a company rather than focusing on one process or project, as well as those who are interested in minute details. Individuals are needed who have broad business knowledge as well as those with an understanding of how management, finance, and IT are run.

Clarify to whom the enterprise architect should report, decide who shall act as the spokesperson, and determine who should have the deciding role in any conflicts that arise between the project's results and the long-term interests of the organization.

Identify the authorizations you need as an enterprise architect to be able to carry out your tasks. Document the points of contact with other decision-making processes in the organization such as project management models.

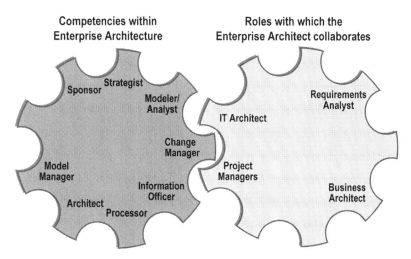

Figure 2.7   This picture illustrates the importance of coordination between the different competencies contributing to the enterprise architecture and other roles.

Describing competence needs and recruiting

Document the organization's competency needs and take an inventory of the competencies that currently exist within the business. Identify any gaps between your inventory and your needs and determine how these should be resolved, whether it be through recruitment or by bringing in consultants. Below, we explain what we mean by competencies (see Figure 2.7):

- **Modeler/Analyst**. Conducts and supervises modeling workshops. Creates new models, conducts analyses, and draws conclusions based on the workshops' results. Deals with processes, information, and matrices.

- **Change manager**. Ensures that EA work is implemented. Deals extensively with leading business operations through the change process. Cultural change is often one of the greatest challenges when working in this role.

- **Strategist**. Works to safeguard the benefit of the EA work in the long term. Work includes identifying EA activities based on the business plan. Works closely with the Informant to identify current business problems for which EA could provide solutions.

- **Processor**. Acts as a "motor" in the architecture process to motivate and impel others. Has a capacity to get things happening and reacts rapidly and pragmatically to initiate new events. Displays leadership qualities and may be the person who convenes meetings and distributes tasks.

- **Sponsor**. A leader who is responsible for continuity. Not directly involved in daily EA work.

- **Model manager**. Manages models and definitions. Supplies projects and business managers with existing models. Publishes, distributes, and manages different versions of the models. Often has a different profile than the modeler, but it is possible for them to be the same person.

- **Architect**. Responsible for the enterprise architecture and its links to management, projects, and the business. Ensures that projects adhere to the intentions of the architecture.

- **Informant**. Understands the benefits of EA and is able to communicate these benefits throughout the organization. If information officers already exist within the organization, it is beneficial to use them instead of creating the Informant role.

The employees with the competencies described above should define how they will interact with IT architects, business architects, project managers, requirements analysts, etc. Use processes to show how they (sponsors, architects, etc.) interact with these roles. The following are examples of processes involving interaction with other roles:

- In long-term business planning, the enterprise architect charts and elaborates proposals that focus on business operations. Following a decision on the proposals, it should be used as the basis for the development of the EA and IT plans.

- In development projects, the people assigned to the competency roles collaborate not only with project managers but also with IT architects so that they can provide checks on everything from requirements specification to systems specification and realization.

Establishing prioritization rules for projects

As the architecture's development moves along, it may become difficult for the enterprise architect to find the time to participate in all of the projects and initiatives pertaining to EA. Consequently, there needs to be a method for prioritizing projects. The projects that are the most important to the business should also be the enterprise architect's main focus.

Here are some possible criteria for establishing the priority of projects:

- Priority of the project within the business plan
- The project's effects on finances
- The size of the project's budget

- If system phase-out plans require extensive commitment
- The complexity of the project
- How the project fits into prioritized areas of the entity group model
- If strategically important processes relate to the project.

One recommendation for forming a prioritization sequence is to define different levels of the architect's commitment to a project and to link a certain level of commitment to the levels of importance listed above (see Figure 2.8).

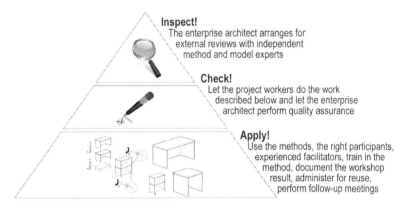

Inspect!
The enterprise architect arranges for external reviews with independent method and model experts

Check!
Let the project workers do the work described below and let the enterprise architect perform quality assurance

Apply!
Use the methods, the right participants, experienced facilitators, train in the method, document the workshop result, administer for reuse, perform follow-up meetings

Figure 2.8   The figure illustrates different ways of working actively as an enterprise architect. Most of the architect's time is devoted to monitoring methods and supplying projects with materials.

Different levels of architectural commitment are given below:

- The enterprise architect does not participate in the project but carries out a number of quality assurance activities, thereby helping to ensure that the results of the project are moving in the right direction. It can be helpful to establish different levels of approval:

  1. Green – Everything looks good, keep up the good work.

2. Yellow – A few minor comments, but the project owner or manager can fix small problems without the need for the architect to carry out a new quality check.

3. Red – The project has such serious shortcomings that measures are needed; a new review should be conducted once the weaknesses have been corrected.

- The enterprise architect is a resource in the project and contributes relevant materials and expertise.

- The architect has complete architectural responsibility. The enterprise architect independently develops an EA plan based on the intentions of the business and its city plan.

It is a good idea to place responsibility for the reduction of redundant information acquisition on the project managers. The projects should be assessed on their contribution to the task of reducing redundancy within the systems. They are also obligated to check their progress against the city plan to ensure that activities are conducted in a manner that safeguards coordination and the reduction of redundancy. The enterprise architect contributes personally to high-priority projects according to the defined criteria. Following are a number of tips on aspects that should be examined.

Information model:
- Layout is aligned with model guidelines (standard positions for Customer, Product, Location, etc.)
- Relations are named moving from the right to the left
- Entities have clear names and are defined
- Event entities exist
- The model is generalized to the extent that it is not specific only to one solution
- The model's contents are ordered in the project directives.

Process model:

- Layout is orderly and understandable
- Start events and results are listed and clearly labeled
- Processes and activities are named using infinitive verbs (place "to" in front of the name) and are uniquely numbered
- There is traceability in the models. It should be easy to follow the main concept from Level 1 to Level 2 in the process model.

Identifying triggers and warnings

As an enterprise architect, you often have to react quickly. Therefore, it is advantageous to consider what triggers an EA event before starting work. A start event can have many causes, linked to both business development and technology shifts. A few examples are given below:

- A new business model canvas and/or strategy is developed.
- A new business system is acquired.
- A new person is appointed to a key decision-making role.
- A company is acquired.
- A new product or way of doing business is introduced.
- A new (unplanned) project is initiated.
- IT development selects a repository for systems development.
- A project runs out of control.
- A new key partner is selected.
- Management chooses an IT partner based on their sector knowledge and their ability to implement new systems.

It is also a good idea to list examples of warning signs of impending problems to which the enterprise architect should react. A few examples are listed below:

- There is a lack of clarity in regards to the business benefits a project should provide and the problems it is intended to resolve.
- A project invents or builds something that already exists. This creates an obvious conflict with the intentions of the city plan, which says that information is acquired only once and is then reused.
- A project is focused too much on getting a specific tool, despite the fact that the end product is designed to support operations only and not processes, entities, or other business descriptions.
- The project has run out of control; it fails to meet schedules or loses participants, the project manager changes, or it becomes necessary to redo work.
- A project repeats its tasks.

Hints

- Define rules in relation to warning signs and list examples.
- Describe the decision-making process.
- Create templates and checklists for decision meetings.

Think about how the warning signs should be handled. The best way to do this is to avoid a situation in which it becomes necessary to stop an initiative. One approach is to formulate early on the risks associated with continuing the project on its initial path. Risks can take several forms, including:

- Reduced flexibility due to becoming locked into structures that prevent change
- Redundant efforts
- Quality shortcomings and problems with the accuracy of information.

2.5 IDENTIFYING REQUIREMENTS FOR EA TOOLS

In the beginning stages of an enterprise architecture process, it is possible to keep track of models and concepts manually. However, as the process continues a situation is quickly reached in which it becomes difficult to manage changes to models and definitions without acquiring some tools to support such management. An EA tool can include all kinds of information, from a business view to an implemented application with all requisite attributes. An EA tool could be a simple drawing tool or a capable one with several functions and a well-defined database. The requirements for the tool should, like any other helpful device, be based on how it is to be used in the EA processes and the information that it needs to manage (the information model). Since setting the requirements involves using EA information about the business's information, this information model has the nature of a meta-model.

Forming meta-models

On the following two pages, examples are given of meta-models describing the entities an enterprise architect needs to manage during the model management process. The first model, shown in Figure 2.9, describes model management and its associated entities. The second model, shown in Figure 2.10, illustrates in detail the meta-entities involved in the enterprise architect's everyday work. It can be beneficial to develop a framework that shows which models you need to manage and the processes that create these models.

This framework can also be used as a basis for prioritizing the models you consider to be the most important to manage within a specific project. In the last chapter, we provide an example of what such a framework may look like.

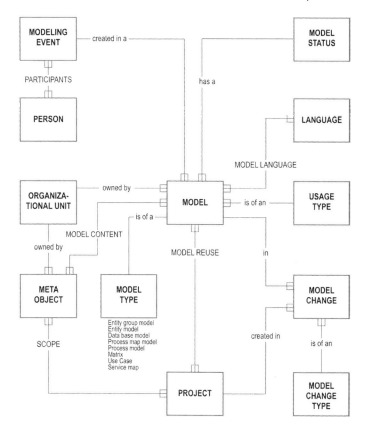

Figure 2.9   Information model of model management; a "meta-model."

Sometimes it is possible to end up in a situation in which some participants are modeling at a detailed level while others are creating models at a more general level. In such cases, it can be useful to use a simplified framework and to agree on which type of model is being developed. The framework of models can also be used in modeling planning. The meta-models, the EA processes, and your improved development process form the requirements for your management tool.

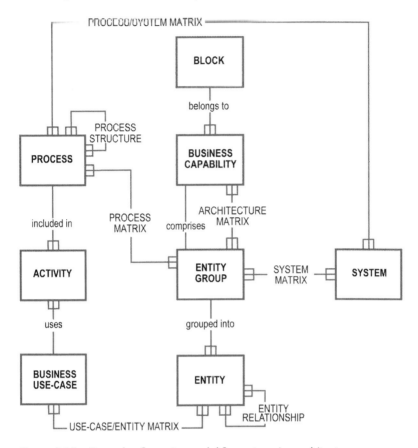

Figure 2.10   Example of a meta-model for enterprise architecture.

In addition to these necessities, ask yourself if the EA tool you are considering can help you answer the following questions:

- How do you want to publish your models?
- What are your requirements for accessing and amending models?
- What are your availability requirements, and what are your security requirements?
- What will be the number of simultaneous users?
- Which people will work with the tool?
- What are the syntax requirements, and are there opportunities to use your own symbols?

- What are the possible demands for being able to make changes in the tool's meta-model?
- What support exists for multiple languages?

Strive for having just one EA tool within your enterprise. Plan for training at several levels within the organization in the use of the tool and inform the stakeholders concerned.

Hints

- Develop a meta-model showing the information to be handled by the tool.
- Establish rules for how the models are to be managed.

Consider the types of models and their level of detail. If you try to include absolutely every bit of information in your models, the tool will quickly be filled with so many detailed models that it will be difficult to maintain an enterprise-wide perspective.

Identifying rules for models

One recommendation for how to maintain a useful-but-not-overwhelming level of detail in your models is to establish a basic layout that determines where elements of the business should be positioned. For example, the organization may be located in one place in information models, event entities in another, and service or product in a third place, as shown in Figure 2.11. It is also advantageous to categorize the entities and use colors to differentiate between them.

Correspondingly, determine how process maps and process models are to be documented. It is recommended that you make a clear distinction between current and future perspectives. Always include the process's start event, result, and customer.

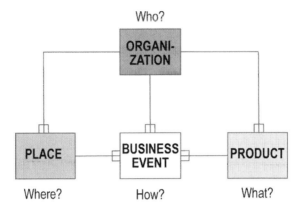

Figure 2.11   Example of basic layout and color standard in an information model. See the information model examples in the previous chapter for more on this layout.

2.6 COMMUNICATING AND PLANNING

When establishing the EA work, there are a few important factors to consider that we would like to emphasize in this chapter. We call them *key success factors.*

Key success factors

A key factor for the success of EA is to provide continuous information to people throughout the organization about the process of establishing an enterprise architecture. Start by describing to the stakeholders how they will be informed about news and progress in the enterprise architecture process. Identify communication channels and decide how often target groups should be informed. Gain an understanding of the target groups' everyday situation so that you know what information they need and how to communicate to them. It can be beneficial to list expected reactions and constructive responses. Provide training for different roles and stakeholders. Sponsors and coaches also need to be trained and given communication materials. They should understand what their roles entail and what is expected of them.

Most importantly, if you want to make changes and get a good return on your EA investment, you need to maintain the enthusiastic participation of all involved parties. Everyone involved needs to be aware of why EA should be used, they must have a desire to use the methods described, and they must have the knowledge and skills necessary for achieving the desired results. Even if they do have the requisite knowledge, it is vital for the organization to have the ability to use that knowledge. In the next chapter, we describe how to act as an EA and how to work with reinforcement.

Hints

- Establish lines of communication about the conclusions and activities discovered in the city plan so that you can start paving the way for the introduction of the city plan concepts.
- Involve senior management in finding entity owners when forming the EA governance model and in communicating the EA message.
- Present planned EA activities to the decision-making forums for the development project.
- Understand how the EA group intends to work and its connections to management, project management, and other stakeholders.

Now we are "Ready" and "Set." Let's "Go"!

Chapter 3
GO

This chapter details the implementation of enterprise architecture. It is about contributing to development projects by focusing on an overall view. In practice, this entails elaborating on the results developed in the city plan, continuing to build support for EA throughout the enterprise and continuously improving on how information is dealt with, the models produced by EA, and its working methods. Summary of activities in *Go*:

Conducting enterprise architecture work in practice:
- Participating in projects
- Working with information models and conceptual models
- Working with information models for the architecture and for requirements specification
- Supporting projects relating to requirements specifications
- Providing support for data origination procedures
- Developing triggers and actions for the enterprise architect
- Managing models
- Communicating target achievements
- Developing standard/generic models.

Improving the EA work:
- Monitoring the external environment
- Fine tuning entities and processes
- Improving regulations.

Figure 3.1   The EA process method focusing on the final stage, Go!

3.1 CONDUCTING ENTERPRISE ARCHITECTURE WORK IN PRACTICE

Participating in projects

The enterprise architect should be service-minded and available to give advice to different parties throughout the enterprise. The architect may lead workshops relating to process mapping, process development, information modeling, and the elaboration of conceptual definitions, and is able to proceed from a superior knowledge platform by using their library of models.

An enterprise architect who has participated in several projects previously has greater business awareness than many people in the organization and is therefore able to contribute by conducting SWOT analyses, benefit assessments and the coordination of project results.

The following is an example of how an architect might participate in project development:

1. The project is initiated.

2. The enterprise architect contacts the project manager in order to become acquainted with the project's problems, solutions, and limitations. The architect reviews the city plan and takes note of any material that could be useful when displayed in information models and with definitions, process models, and matrices.

3. Together, the project manager and enterprise architect delineate the project's boundaries in the process map and entity group models and map ongoing projects in order to identify possible overlaps (see Figure 3.2).

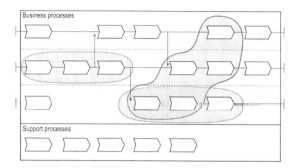

Figure 3.2   Example showing three project scopes.

4. The project manager is provided with guidelines regarding its scope and results. The enterprise architect informs the project manager about the EA governance model and the entity managers and forums in particular.

5. The project's workers are supplied with previous results that have the potential to be reused. Together, the project workers and the enterprise architect discuss the project's expected results, and this information is relayed back to the enterprise architect.

6. Integration guidelines concerning sourcing and how to reuse information are discussed. In many cases, the process of phasing out systems is also included in the scope of the project.

7. The project team decides and plans the enterprise architect's level of commitment in the project, which can include the following:

    a. Making existing results available, such as process and information models
    b. Performing a number of quality assurance activities
    c. Acting as a resource for the project
    d. Taking on complete responsibility for the architecture.

It is a good idea for the enterprise architect to contact project managers and project teams so that the enterprise architects can offer services to these groups. For example, the architect can help to pick out relevant material, participate in project meetings, and deliver models and definitions that are already available. Encourage the project leader to use models and to tackle structural challenges so that the solutions to the project's challenges benefit the whole organization. The project leader is also provided with method instructions and checkpoints. Reward projects that set a good example. Appropriate rewards include giving recognition by awarding titles such as "project team of the year" or benefits such as a half-day off for all project members.

Projects in which the enterprise architect has a lower level of commitment (for example, projects concerning information areas or processes that do not have a significant impact on the enterprise as a whole) should be subject to planned reviews by the architect. These reviews consist of examining the processes, information models, concepts, matrices, and other elements of the architecture to ensure that they meet the predetermined quality requirements. For example, the architect should make sure that the project's models are comprehensible, accurate, and correctly drawn, and that they demonstrate that the project is on the right track.

The enterprise architect can also check to see that the standardized structures are adhered to and can identify situations in which the standards and quality require improvement. The architect also checks that the project's guidelines are followed and that the planned reuse, coordination, integration, and phase-out steps take place. Both the enterprise architect and the project team should be aware of what needs to be done in the event of any deficiencies. The architect should primarily help the project achieve enhanced quality and, as a last resort, use his or her position of authority and expertise to make corrections.

The day-to-day behavior of the enterprise architect is just as important as his or her knowledge is to the success of the EA efforts, as shown in Figure 3.3. The architect who contributes to projects is much more appreciated than one who assumes the role of auditor or policeman. An enterprise architect who inspires is invited to participate more often than is one who assumes a questioning stance. The architect should take the problems faced by the recipient as the starting point when promoting architectural concepts rather than trying to promote just an EA perspective. An enterprise architect should take a leading role in high-priority areas and assist in lower-priority areas by preparing materials and following up on results.

To be able to contribute to projects with materials developed earlier or by other projects, it is necessary to keep models and concepts organized. Consequently, a key part of the enterprise architect's everyday work involves administering the entire city plan and developing it further. Keep demonstrating EA's benefits by using the collected enterprise architect measurements.

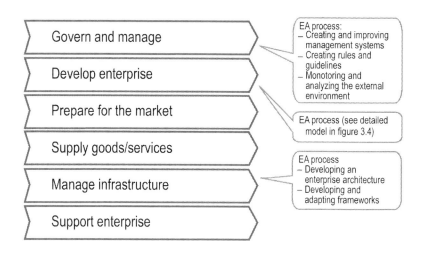

Figure 3.3   This shows, in general terms, where the enterprise architect operates.

Show that the business is better prepared to deal with new requirements imposed on it by the external environment and issue reminders to people throughout the organization when events that reflect this change occur. These may seem like unnecessary activities, but it is quite common for project workers to want to work within just a project scope to shorten lead team. It is therefore good to remind them of the benefits of reusing earlier material.

An enterprise architect is involved in developing business operations as well as in the management and support processes. These operations and processes need to be described so that the efforts of the enterprise architect become obvious and enable higher information quality and reuse of information. See Figure 3.4.

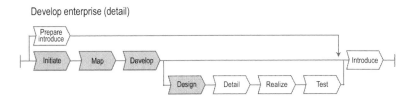

Develop enterprise (detail)

Figure 3.4   Detailed model of the "Develop enterprise" process. The enterprise architect is primarily involved in the initiate, map, develop, and design processes (marked gray).

Working with information models and conceptual models

As mentioned previously, there are at least two main motivations for producing an information model:

1. Ensuring that important business information and rules are captured
2. Obtaining a view of business information that helps IT to produce a database model.

An information model shows how entities correspond to important enterprise concepts and how these concepts relate to one another. What, then, is an entity? According to our definition, it is something:

- That is crucial to the enterprise
- That can be uniquely identified
- That holds information that needs to be managed
- That has occurrences (e.g. the entity CUSTOMER has the occurrences "Customer 1 – John Svensson", "Customer 2 – Kate Ericson").

An information model should be constructed in a workshop with the participation of individuals with knowledge of their specific business sector. Begin the workshop by defining the key enterprise concepts and deciding which of these concepts should be classified as entities. This decision-making process determines the relationships between different entities (one-to-one relationships, one-to-many relationships, and many-to-many relationships). Some examples of entities include Customer Order, Agreement, Product, and Material. See Figure 3.5.

One should avoid identifying documents, such as price lists and delivery notes, as entities. Documents of this kind contain a number of entities that need to be defined. For example, a price list is probably dependent on the entities *Product Components*, *Market*, *Customer*, and maybe even sales volumes based on *Customer Orders*, and is therefore not an entity in itself.

Sometimes information modeling is not conceivable outside the domain of IT. Business representatives may be intimidated by its complexity and may even refuse to participate in the modeling process. In this case, working with conceptual models rather than information models is a more feasible course of action.

Normalized information model

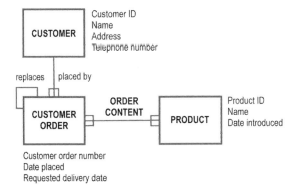

Conceptual model

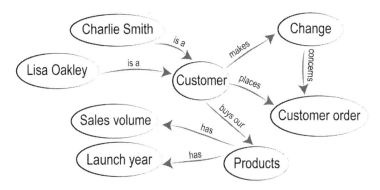

Figure 3.5   The picture shows an example of both an information model and a conceptual model.

Conceptual models are usually used to clarify terminology between groups of people and are also an effective way to capture business terms in workshops. A conceptual model does not need to have defined relationship connections, such as one-to-many, between concepts, and its concepts are not required to have unique instances.

Consequently, concepts such as sales volume, launch year, change, and the Charlie Smith are example of conceptual terms that would not qualify as entities. While compilations, instances, functions, attributes, and documents may appear in a conceptual model, they do not qualify for inclusion in an information model, as it contains only entities and relationships. Entities are very basic, a property that makes them more sustainable. In some cases, a conceptual model may be a practical precursor to an information model, examples shown in Figure 3.6

Concepts in a Concept Model	Could be the following Entities in an Information Model
Sales Statistics	Customer, Customer Order, Product, Market
Minutes	Meeting (or perhaps Decision)
Case Number	Case
Budget	Cost Center, Budgeted Cost, Period

Figure 3.6   Examples of differences between conceptual models and information models.

Working with information models for the architecture and for requirements specification

Information models describing the enterprise architecture need to be generalized to a certain extent in order for the architecture to be flexible and future-proof. The reason for generalizing models is to capture business requirements and ensure that the model is based on future situations without being locked into the limitations that currently prevail. An information model at the architectural level should have a global view of the enterprise along with clear definitions that can be understood throughout the organization. The purpose with this kind of model is to have a future-proof model that comes from an enterprise perspective.

When specifying requirements for a certain business area or project by using an information model, begin the specification process by looking at the business's needs. Although it is a good idea to start by looking at the architecture models, these models are not detailed enough for this purpose. It is advantageous to model phenomena that are unique to a certain business process so that definitions specific to the requirement's needs are established. An information model of this kind is often quite detailed. The entities' names do not need to take on a global perspective in requirements contexts and can instead be more specific to the area for which the requirements are specified. Requirements projects often invest more energy into specifying new entities for future processes and event entities, while devoting less time to common resource and category entities.

An enterprise architect must be able to work from the architecture as well as from the requirements perspectives. When a specific requirements specification is completed, the enterprise architect should take a stance on the following issues:

- Whether enterprise-wide entities conform to agreed-upon standards
- What entities in the requirements specification should be included in the city plan
- Whether entities and definitions in this specification need to be generalized or improved upon in order to become future-proof.

Supporting projects relating to requirements specifications

The enterprise architect should participate directly in the requirements specification work for the strategically important entity groups and processes. For other projects, it may be sufficient for the architect to conduct checks or reviews according to the EA governance model.

When a project's focus shifts onto systems specification and realization, the enterprise architect's involvement diminishes and only reappears in the final stage of project development. Current models should be re-entered into the city plan so that it can continue to develop and increase in its level of detail. However, it is important to consider the level of the models to be re-entered. If all process and information models are re-entered from the requirements specification, one would quickly drown in models that also vary in their level of detail.

Therefore, establish rules in regards to the degree and level of detail of the information to be re-entered at the *Set* stage and follow these guidelines when recycling information models and mapping them against the city plan.

Providing support for systems acquisitions

In connection with systems acquisitions, the enterprise architect may contribute to mapping systems to the business information structure.

A requirements specification is usually included in a RFQ (Request For Quotation). In assessing responses from suppliers, it is useful to use all of the specification documentation. Your analysis will be improved significantly by mapping the information model against the suppliers' system data models, an example being shown in Figure 3.7.

Determine what the supplier is able to manage currently, is able to manage with certain adaptations, and is unable to manage. Use colors to visually separate these three categories in your reference model. Often the supplier has only a "raw," tabular description that must be translated into comprehensible information before the mapping of the supplier's capabilities against the requirements information model can be completed.

Do not forget to compare your future processes with the supplier's current processes. If there are any discrepancies between the two, a decision should be made in regards to whether the supplier's processes should be implemented or if adaptations should be made to the processes.

1. Incomprehensible database model

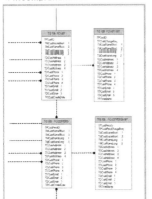

2. Comprehensible Information model of the system

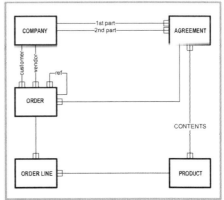

3. Mapping – information covered by the system

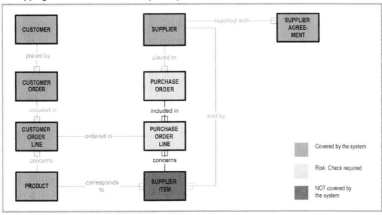

Figure 3.7   The figure shows examples of a description from a supplier (upper left), an information model (upper right), and how a mapping between requirements and system can be documented (lower left).

The systems and entity group matrix provides an excellent basis on which to ascertain integration needs. If the supplier's system requires that they produce information that already exists in the enterprise's current systems, a decision must be made about whether to duplicate information acquisition, phase-out the existing system, integrate the two systems, or require that the supplier make adaptations.

Keep the information model secret from the supplier until you have had the opportunity to see the supplier's model. It is common for a supplier, perhaps lacking a model for their own system, to be overly inspired by the requirements specification model and therefore just copy it without having the solutions for such a model.

Developing triggers and actions

Here is a list of common triggers for an enterprise architect, along with the architect's necessary actions:

Trigger: a start date for a project is reached

The enterprise architect or project manager initiates the development procedures that were established in the development and phase-out plan (or elsewhere). The enterprise architect should pick up at an early stage on projects that are about to be started. Contact the project's manager before his or her tasks are completed and select relevant materials for the project scope in the form of process models, information models and definitions, and interactions with other projects. Together with the project manager, formulate a plan for the enterprise architect's assistance and contact the relevant information owners.

Trigger: a project runs out of control

An enterprise architect should act quickly when he or she sees that a project is failing to meet deadlines, loses participants, changes its project manager, or has to perform the same task two or more times. Conduct a diagnosis of the project by disregarding any personnel-related problems and return to the project's original expectations. Decide what is needed for the project to succeed. It is preferable to provide assistance as opposed to stopping the project if its intentions are worthwhile.

In the previous chapter, *Set*, criteria were described for when a business improvement initiative should be stopped using the enterprise architect's mandate. As a service-minded and proactive enterprise architect, it should not be necessary to exercise this mandate in order to stop a project. If this is nonetheless unavoidable, it is necessary to be well prepared for the possibility that the stop might fail and the enterprise architect's authority will be negatively affected. Therefore, be sure that this "emergency brake" is not applied capriciously. Review the project thoroughly, collect arguments and find facts to support them, and determine the effects of ending the project on the enterprise's architecture and employees. Use the decision-making forum defined in the EA governance model.

Plan the timing of the stop carefully. Consider who should be informed and by whom and with what wording. Prepare for different reactions from people and decide beforehand how you will deal with them. Implement the stop and gather together materials from the project that can be reused in the future. Follow up on how and why the stop took place and be sincere in learning from the experience. Highlight the initiative's successful aspects and emphasize them. In the long term, the most successful course of action is, of course, to avoid dramatic use of the architect's project mandate.

Hints

- Do your best to avoid stopping a project! Do so only if there are no other alternatives.
- Follow up on and communicate with project leaders about any problems that arise. Be sure to learn from your mistakes.

Trigger: a new business model, strategy, or plan is published

The board of directors has adopted one or more new business models and has set new courses for the achievement of business entities. The business entities may have also been changed. This requires that the enterprise architect become acquainted with the new guidelines, consider how they affect EA strategy, and, where necessary, update current initiatives and disseminate this new information. This process may lead to significant changes in the EA plan and ongoing projects. Each project should be reassessed, and the enterprise architect should confirm that each project actually undergoes this assessment.

Trigger: a new ERP system is acquired

Management has decided to introduce an ERP (enterprise resource planning) system because it represents the best practice, solutions, and standards for a certain sector and should be utilized as much as possible. In this situation, it may seem unnecessary to construct processes and information models for the organization's own operations, but it is, in fact, particularly important to chart current processes and the desired future situation in relation to current entities and visions. These future processes should be compared with the ERP system's processes that will allow management to see, in a controlled manner, what is conforming to the preferred way of working and what is not. The same applies for entities and relationships between entities that show business rules.

If the entities and the relationships between them are critical to conducting operations successfully, these must be compared to the system's information model. This comparison also provides clear documentation for management. It shows where special solutions should be implemented in order to avoid surprises following the introduction of the new system. The matrices included in the city plan are also useful for showing the order suitable for the introduction of the ERP system and the existing integration requirements. Consequently, having an updated city plan is crucial, and it should be used actively in the acquisition and introduction of ERP systems.

Trigger: a new or updated business plan is published

The president or director of the business has updated a business plan for a certain amount of time (one year, three years, etc.). In many instances, the enterprise architect has been a member of the business plan's development committee and has described how EA will contribute to the business and its entities. In such cases, the business plan provides a communications channel for the enterprise architect. The plan includes ideas for meeting needs within the organization and descriptions of what needs to be done in the near future. Helping to establish the new business plan allows the enterprise architect to be proactive and enter the project at a very early stage.

Trigger: a new person is appointed to a key decision-making role

When a senior manager changes jobs, another area opens up in which the enterprise architect can have an impact. Maintain your relationship with the senior manager even when he or she moves to a new position with new areas of responsibility and try to establish a relationship with his or her successor. Research the most effective ways to promote EA to the manager's successor, compile examples of how EA contributed to his or her predecessor's success, and give a presentation on your examples. Begin your talk with what interests that person rather than with what would interest an enterprise architect.

Trigger: a company is acquired

When the enterprise architect learns that a company will be acquired, it is of great benefit to ascertain, from the beginning, the intentions behind the acquisition. This helps the architect to judge how the acquisition will affect the architecture. If the operations of the new company are to be integrated into existing operations, a quick city plan and a special development and phase-out plan should be created for the new company.

In this situation, speed takes precedence over comprehensiveness, so a rudimentary entity group model and process map may be sufficient. These can be based on interviews and enquiries from open sources about the company, or they can be derived from standard or generic models (such as Silverston's Universal Models). Try to understand the company's customer values, key success factors, and the key areas of its systems map. Make a comparison with the acquiring company's overall city plan, as well as its development and phase-out plan, and identify common areas between the two organizations' plans. Plan and carry out a meeting with those responsible for the integration of the new company. Take this opportunity to be of service and to offer EA expertise. Identify those interested in architecture in the new company and begin establishing relationships with them.

Trigger: a new product or way of doing business is introduced

A decision is made to invest in the development of an entirely new product that will be on the periphery of the business's current product line. The enterprise architect should have a good relationship with the company's business and process developers. Together, the business and process developers can work together with the enterprise architect to find ways to work with the development of the new product. The enterprise architect can, for instance, talk about the benefits of the new offering by using a Business Model Canvas. The architect is also able to contribute models of processes and information assets and can ensure that the ideas that are implemented in the development process of the new product are realistic. In return, the enterprise architect learns early on about dramatic changes in processes and gains new sources of information.

Trigger: a new (unplanned) project is initiated

Despite well-structured architecture work and controlled initiatives, projects that are not covered by the development and phase-out plan do arise. People with integrity and a progressive spirit place orders and initiate projects with good intentions, but they may do so solely to meet the needs of their part of the organization. The enterprise architect may, for example, learn that a standard package for human resource operations is to be acquired or that a consultancy company has been hired to build a data warehouse (OLAP), and that they have applied to collect data from a particular system. Significant unplanned events include management deciding on which ERP system will be chosen to replace 20 central systems.

The same management that once approved the current development and phase-out plan may now be making a decision that counteracts their previous plans. In all of these situations, it is necessary for the enterprise architect to be thorough in their preparations, compile arguments, check through the library of models, and collect materials that the project should be able to use. With the right timing and attitude, the enterprise architect can fulfill the demands of the person placing the order, the project manager and, possibly, an external supplier to assess the benefits and opportunities that may arise from the new project. As long as there are tangible benefits to carrying out the project, do not consider stopping the initiative simply because it was unplanned. Since the enterprise architect is reactive in this context, it becomes even more important for him or her to be ready to serve rather than look like someone who is holding the project back.

Trigger: a new systems development method is selected

Research the method and identify how it interfaces with EA results such as information models, process maps, and matrices. Establish relations with people who are knowledgeable about the new method and ensure that it fits in well with the current development and phase-out plan, process models, information models, and matrices.

Trigger: a new key partner needs to be chosen by management

Develop future processes that show how interactions with the new partner will take place. Establish the customary process and systems matrices. Decide, together with the partner, how operational information is to be captured and disseminated so that it is easy to determine what systems and services should be used. Consider how the day-to-day operational processes should be followed up on and measured.

Managing models

Many enterprises have already acquired powerful tools, such as dictionaries or repositories, and have used them to collect all of the organization's produced models. Little time is available to become familiar with the models and to determine which are of architectural value and which are only of interest for a particular area of the business. Consequently, it is important to establish rules regarding which models will be saved in the tool. This is discussed in greater detail in the previous chapter.

The amount of time and effort put into developing models grows in scope as more models are established and more perspectives are included (from management, operations, requirements, design, solution, etc.). Review the developed requirements specifications and adopt a method for determining which models should be merged into the city plan and at what level the information should be saved in the repository.

Communicating target achievements

Measurable EA targets need to be communicated to everyone working on the architecture as EA's results begin to become discernible in the organization. It is crucial to be able to demonstrate the benefits of an enterprise-wide architecture, and, for this reason, constant measurements must be made. Adhere to the communications plan and make corrections where necessary. Too many EA offices have been closed because they failed to demonstrate their achievements.

Continuously measure both the effects of the EA work and its performance. Keep assessment forms on hand and ask for opinions from project participants, project assignors, workshop participants, and others who have worked on your activities. Collect and review suggestions for improvement. One way to do this is to capture each project's expectations of what enterprise architecture will provide and follow up on the project members' opinions once the project has been completed.

Developing standard/generic models

The enterprise architect works to establish standardized structures such as a customer identifier and structure, a product definition structure, or just an identifier for an asset. A standard structure can also be a relatively substantial model applicable to, for example, master data for human resources or a target structure for a data warehouse. The enterprise architect can push standardization efforts forwards and collect requirements from various stakeholders. A standard should be included in the EA governance model.

3.2 IMPROVING THE EA WORK

Monitoring the external environment

An enterprise architect should stay up to date on achievements within the field of EA. They can do this by subscribing to newspapers, magazines, and newsletters; attending conferences; participating in networks; and searching for new literature in order to gain an impression of how others have succeeded and learned from their successes and failures. It is advantageous to share your experiences at network meetings and conferences. Talking about your own situation with others often enhances self-awareness and gives rise to new ideas.

Fine-tuning entities and processes

Review processes in which the enterprise architect is active. Fine-tune the EA objectives, identify new measures, and increase your expectations if you have achieved your original goals. Review the activities and compare your observations with project teams and stakeholders. Ensure that the support structure—in the shape of checklists, templates, standard agendas and role descriptions—is up to date.

Improving regulations

Continue working with the governance model by clarifying who EA's customers are and by assessing its customer values, deliverables, and service levels. Establish and re-assess the EA issues that need to be addressed by the appropriate forum and review how decisions on these issues are raised and monitored. Adjust the model's mandate if necessary. Make sure that architectural activities are included in the development processes and that there are descriptions in the processes about how the architecture results are to be used.

Hints

- Fine-tune the EA process and set new goals.
- Stay up-to-date in the field of EA
- Communicate your target achievements to the organization.

Ready, Set, and here we Go!

Note that for more on our framework, please read the following Appendix.

Appendix
THE ZACHMAN FRAMEWORK AND OUR EA PROCESS

The thoughts expressed in this book are, in many senses, based the Zachman Framework. Figure 4.1 shows the Zachman Framework 3.0 (excluding the details). You can view the entire framework at www.zachmaninternational.com.

John F. Zachman developed this framework in the 1980s, and it is widely used in both public and private sectors all over the world. It may be compared to the periodic table of the elements in that it provides a systematic, visual display of an enterprise.

The Zachman Framework for Enterprise Architecture™
The Enterprise Ontology™

Version 3.0 *Simplified*

	What	How	Where	Who	When	Why	
Executive Perspective *(Business Context Planners)*	Inventory Identification	Process Identification	Distribution Identification	Responsibility Identification	Timing Identification	Motivation Identification	Scope Contexts *(Scope Identification Lists)*
Business Management Perspective *(Business Concept Owners)*	Inventory Definition	Process Definition	Distribution Definition	Responsibility Definition	Timing Definition	Motivation Definition	Business Concepts *(Business Definition Models)*
Architect Perspective *(Business Logic Designers)*	Inventory Representation	Process Representation	Distribution Representation	Responsibility Representation	Timing Representation	Motivation Representation	System Logic *(System Representation Models)*
Engineer Perspective *(Business Physics Builders)*	Inventory Specification	Process Specification	Distribution Specification	Responsibility Specification	Timing Specification	Motivation Specification	Technology Physics *(Technology Specification Models)*
Technician Perspective *(Business Component Implementers)*	Inventory Configuration	Process Configuration	Distribution Configuration	Responsibility Configuration	Timing Configuration	Motivation Configuration	Tool Components *(Tool Configuration Models)*
Enterprise Perspective *(Users)* The Enterprise	Inventory Instantiations	Process Instantiations	Distribution Instantiations	Responsibility Instantiations	Timing Instantiations	Motivation Instantiations	Operation Instances *(Implementation)* The Enterprise
	Inventory Sets	Process Flows	Distribution Networks	Responsibility Assignments	Timing Cycles	Motivation Intentions	

Figure 4.1   Overview   of   the   Zachman   framework.   Source: www.zachmaninternational.com. Used with permission.

According to John F. Zachman, there is a model in each cell of the framework, whether this has been written down or not. Additionally, Zachman takes the view that it is possible to contain a model within a single cell. If a model flows over into several cells, it becomes less efficient. This means that, for example, a process description should only show how an operation is conducted and not how it is organized. Similarly, in order for an information model to be useful, it should be free of systems, processes, and organization.

Because the framework is quite extensive, we, the authors, have chosen to include in this book only the parts that are the most useful for the purposes of enterprise architecture and business development. Most senior management teams primarily want an answer to the question "Why?" (that is, Zachman's Motivation column), which is our reason for placing the Motivation column first. According to Zachman, there is no internal order among the columns. The order in which they are presented is optional. The sections about modeling presented in this book, and in practice in our assignments, are based on the Zachman Framework principles although we chose the parts from the framework for which there is a need for modeling. Figure 4.2 shows a sample application of the Zachman Framework. The columns are the same as the original framework, but in addition to Zachman's roles representing each row in the framework, we have introduced processes since a process can include many roles.

Figure 4.2 shows the processes that produce and maintain different models. The Business Model Canvas is used to express and capture business innovations. Such a model violates the Zachman principle about having a model diagram reflecting only one cell since a canvas reflects many cells within one perspective. In order to express how an innovation is implemented by the enterprise architecture, there need to be specifications about how business processes, information, and organization models affect the implementation. Those models reflect how a business is formed (see the Operate row and Change row in Figure 4.2).

The Zachman Framework 3.0 adopted by the Authors

Process	why	how	what	who	where	when	Perspective
Innovate	Business Model Canvas						Executive
Operate	Business Vision & Strategy	Business Process Model	Business Information Model	Organziation & Roles	Geographical model		Business management
Change	Improvement expectations						Architecture
Design	Solution visions	Use case	Database model	Role permissions	Logical network & components		Engineer
Build	IT visions	Service solution	Physical data model	Authorisation	Physical network & components		Technician

Figure 4.2   An example of mapping models and processes to the Zachman Framework.

In practice, modeling becomes more interesting when you start making changes. Too often, we see different kinds of models, such as use cases, logical data (base) models, being formed from a blank paper when designing and building information systems (row Design and Build in Figure 4.2). These models should be derived from corresponding business models. For example, a logical data model should be derived from a business information model, and the use cases should be able to be traced back to a business process model.

Further Reading

Hoberman, S. (2009). <u>Data Modeling Made Simple, 2nd Edition</u>. Technics Publications.

Hoberman, S., Burbank, D., Bradley, C. (2009). <u>Data Modeling for the Business</u>. Technics Publications.

M. Hiatt, J. (2006). <u>ADKAR: A Model for Change in Business, Government and our Community.</u> Prosci Research.

Minoli, D. (2008). <u>Enterprise Architecture A to Z: Frameworks, Business Process Modeling, SOA, and Infrastructure Technology</u>. Auerbach Publications.

Osterwalder, A. (2010). <u>Business Model Generation: A Handbook for Visionaries, Game Challengers, and Challengers</u>. John Wiley & Sons.

P. English, L. (1999). <u>Improving Data Warehouse and Business Information Quality: Methods for Reducing Costs and Increasing Profit</u>. John Wiley & Sons.

Potts, C. (2010). <u>RecrEAtion: Realizing the Extraordinary Contribution of Your Enterprise Architects</u>. Technics Publications.

Schekkerman, J. (2006). <u>How to Survive in the Jungle of Enterprise Architecture Frameworks: Creating or Choosing an Enterprise Architecture Framework</u>. Trafford Publishing.

Silverston, L. (2001). <u>The Data Model Resource Book: A Library of Universal Data Models for All Enterprises</u>. John Wiley & Sons.

Simsion, G. (2004). <u>Data Modeling Essentials, 3rd Edition</u>. Elsevier Science & Technology.

W. Ross, J., Weil, P., C. Robertson, D. (2006). <u>Enterprise Architecture As Strategy: Creating a Foundation for Business Execution</u>. Harvard Business School Press.

Index

Made in the USA
San Bernardino, CA
23 September 2017